DIRECTING THEATER 101

D1319643

DIRECTING THEATER 101

10 STEPS

to Successful Productions
for New Directors and
Regional Theater Companies

WILMA MARCUS CHANDLER

SMITH AND KRAUS
Hanover, New Hampshire

A Smith and Kraus Book
Published by Smith and Kraus, Inc.
177 Lyme Road, Hanover, NH 03755
www.SmithandKraus.com

First Edition: November 2008

Manufactured in the United States of America
10 9 8 7 6 5 4 3 2 1

Book production by Julia Gignoux, Freedom Hill Design
Text and cover design by Kate Mueller, Electric Dragon Productions

Library of Congress Control Number: 2008935713
ISBN-13: 978-1-57525-583-5 / ISBN-10 1-57525-583-9

To all young directors getting ready to
accept the challenge

And to John Chandler,
great husband, writer, critic, and a good actor, too!

Art is not a thing. It is a way.
OSCAR WILDE, POET, PLAYWRIGHT

Contents

STEP 3

How to Read a Play
The First Reading
The Second Reading
Analysis of *The Rising of the Moon*

STEP 4

Dedication
Concept
Basic Staging
Monologues and Soliloquies
Two-Person Scenes
Three-Person Scenes
Four-Person Scenes
Group Scenes
Notes about Rhythm, Tempo, and Arc
What the Actor Needs to Do
Writing It All Down

STEP 5

Royalties
Venue
The Production Book
Research
Budget

STEP 6

STEP 7

STEP 8

STEP 9

STEP 10

Appendix

Introduction

Directing for the theatre may be described as the process of transforming personal vision into public performance.
J. Robert Wills, *The Director in a Changing Theatre*

The director must cultivate the virtue of patience—with others and with himself.
Harold Clurman, *On Directing*

The director is justified in his impatience.
Bertolt Brecht

So we begin with some big ideas. And sometimes these ideas can seem directly opposite to each other. This book is meant to start you on the path toward understanding the work of the theater director and those who work alongside the director.

Directing can be an amazing opportunity for creative expression and personal growth. It can also be a challenge at almost every step along the way. The complex worlds of playwrights, artists, performers, and technicians all emerge and then seemingly, by magic, merge into a production that lifts the words off the page and onto the stage for audiences to enjoy.

But the magic is only the surface. What lies beneath is devotion to the actual work and a passionate commitment to excellence. We have to be burning with excitement and energy to do it! And before that we have to learn how to do it!

I have tried to put into these pages all the basic elements I could think of to get you started on the journey. These are elements I have worked with over the years as a theater director, actor, playwright, and teacher. A lot of the topics I mention are topics I have wrestled with myself.

Keep in mind that taking leadership as a director can be thrilling, but it can also be be frightening. There's a lot to deal with and a lot to learn. I've never started a show without feeling in awe of the material and very scared of the tasks ahead. Can I actually make this work? Can I direct a show? Can I take direction? Do I fully understand what has to happen here?

The director is responsible for almost all the artistic decisions in a production. You are being watched, observed, and sometimes criticized. You are demonstrating how you work in the world and how you communicate with others. You take the blame if things are a mess, but you also take the credit for things that go well at the rehearsals and, at last, on opening night. You also take the credit for a happy cast and crew who feel appreciated and whose talents have been acknowledged.

Those being directed—the actors, staff, and crew—are responsible for listening carefully and using their own creativity to bring forth the director's vision of the world that is the play. So besides being frightening, it can also be a wonderful adventure. What seemed like magic can actually be understood, inch by inch, step by step.

Directing for the theater gives you the chance to explore your thoughts, opinions, and values about life, and then share them with others in a climate of vitality. Who you are is totally unique, and how you see the world is important. Directing gives you the opportunity to go right into the center of your life and into the heart of your ideas.

There are many wonderful books on directing and many paths toward educating yourself to become a theater director. The final chapter provides a guide for you to continue your training and a suggestion of material to read and from which to learn.

Most of all, as you start this work, trust yourself and be brave. Take some risks, make a few mistakes, have patience, lose your patience, and, most of all, have a great time! I hope you will use this book as the first step on a long and rewarding journey.

Wilma Marcus Chandler
Santa Cruz, California, 2008

STEP 1

OVERVIEW OF THEATER

There are no accidents in art . . . only the fruits of long labor.

KONSTANTIN STANISLAVSKI,
MOSCOW ART THEATER DIRECTOR

What equipment does a director need? It's so complicated. You have to be able to use other people as your instrumentality. This is an art in itself—to make your imagination proceed through the imaginations of other people.

ZELDA FICHANDLER, *THE DIRECTOR'S VOICE*

THE NATURE OF THEATER

I believe that theater is the most powerful art form we have and the most exhilarating. At its best, it is a seamless blend of literature, dance, music, art, and politics. It reflects on humanity's great issues and problems and joys. It attempts to build a bridge between performers and audience to reflect on the human experience, and it includes playwrights, poets, designers, business managers, and many others. It is as diverse as the countries and societies in which it is performed, but it is universal as well.

What are the common threads? Theater always speaks to the human heart as well as to the mind. At the center is always a conflict, and that conflict is expressed and resolved through dialogue and action. Theater addresses who we are, what we laugh and cry about, what we have experienced and wish for in the world.

1

So, when you work in the theater, what are you getting your-self into? As with all the arts, theater work requires training to develop the skills necessary to become excellent, and in the performing arts you take big risks. You agree to be looked at, applauded, or booed and have your artistic decisions challenged. But it is also a high form of play that can delight, amaze, and teach an audience many things.

The process always begins with the literature. Playwriting starts the process, and performance lights it up and demonstrates it. Even the spontaneous work of improvisation begins with a subject, a topic, or an audience suggestion to begin a scene.

It is about people on a stage telling their stories and their secrets while other people watch. Hopefully, the audience will be able to empathize and will be moved to laughter, terror, delight, or tears by what they see and hear. Theater is about ideas, characters, and situations. It is about the comedy and the drama of human situations and the whole panorama of the world in which we live.

THE THEATER PRODUCTION TEAM: WHO DOES WHAT?

Theater production relies on a collaboration among many people. No one person can do it all. The director must oversee the entire team and work closely with the producer and the stage manager to keep things on track. Here is a partial list of the collaborators:

THE PLAYWRIGHT writes the play.

THE PRODUCER selects the play, finds the financial backing, and usually hires all the people who will work on the show. The producer can be a school, a theater company, an individual, or a group of individuals.

THE DIRECTOR interprets the script, creates the concept for the show, stages the show, and directs the actors.

THE ASSISTANT DIRECTOR helps the director in all ways and is prepared to take over should the director not be able to continue with the rehearsals or with the production.

THE DRAMATURG does research on the literary, historical, and biographical material in the script and assists the director, designers, and actors with the findings to help them understand the context of the play.

THE PRODUCTION MANAGER deals with schedules, rehearsal time lines, and administrative details.

THE STAGE MANAGER, at first, assists the director, helps with auditions, writes down the blocking notes, takes charge of all backstage operations, and organizes and calls the cues for lights, sound, and scenery shifts. Later, once the show opens, he or she is in charge of the show completely.

THE DESIGNERS (set designer, lighting designer, sound designer, and costume designer) are responsible for creating the artistic designs of the show.

THE SCENIC ARTIST designs the painted scenery and props.

THE PAINT CREW does the actual painting.

THE PROPERTIES MASTER designs, builds, or finds all the props for the show.

THE PROPS CREW helps the prop master and organizes and runs all the props before and during a show.

THE LIGHT-BOARD OPERATOR AND SOUNDBOARD OPERATOR set up and run the equipment during the show; receive cues from the stage manager.

THE MASTER ELECTRICIAN hangs, focuses, and checks the lights according to the lighting designer's plans.

THE ELECTRICIANS work on the stage lighting and wiring for the show.

THE STAGE CREW/RUNNING CREW are the backstage team in charge of moving and changing the sets and props during rehearsals and performances.

THE COSTUME SHOP SUPERVISOR is responsible for making the costumes according to the costume designer's drawings and organizing the costume shop.

THE COSTUME CREW cuts, drapes, and stitches costumes; makes wigs; organizes makeup; and cares for shoes, hats, and so on.

THE DRESSERS assist actors backstage with costume and makeup changes.

THE MUSICAL DIRECTOR is in charge of live music (orchestra, band) for the show.

THE VOCAL DIRECTOR is in charge of singers and rehearsing the songs for the show and coordinates with the musical director.

THE CHOREOGRAPHER creates any dances that may be needed in the show. Also may be asked to stage parts of the show that require special physical movement, such as crowd scenes or fights.

THE DANCE CAPTAIN runs the dance rehearsals and leads warm-ups before rehearsals and performances.

THE FIGHT CHOREOGRAPHER creates the movements necessary for fights in a show, both armed and unarmed, and should be certified or highly trained.

THE WEAPONS MASTER is in charge of checking simulated weapons used in a play before and after each performance, locking them away, and distributing them to the proper actors for each subsequent performance.

THE DIALECT COACH works with actors on the necessary speech inflections and pronunciation for regional or foreign accents.

THE ACTORS, DANCERS, AND SINGERS are the performers.

THE UNDERSTUDIES learn the roles of the actors and should be prepared to go onstage in the absence of a performer.

THE PUBLICITY DIRECTOR is in charge of publicity, posters, photography, programs, advertising, lobby display, and all manner of notifying the public about the production.

THE HOUSE MANAGER is in charge of the theater space: keeping it clean and ready for the public and overseeing ushers and ticket takers; deals with the safety and well-being of the audience.

Often one person will take on several jobs, but doing a show is always a group effort and needs everyone's talents and strengths to run smoothly. The wonderful thing about a production is that every person who wishes to be part of it can find a place. Some have skills in one area, some in another, but there is room for all.

THE DIRECTOR'S ROLES

It is good to remember that nobody asked us to go on the stage. For my own part I elected to do so. And having done that, it is for me to command all my resources by my Will, in order to prove my right to stand there and play!

MORRIS CARNOVSKY, *THE ACTOR'S EYE*

How you work in the world is how you work on stage.

UTA HAGEN, *RESPECT FOR ACTING*

Whether you are becoming a director or working with one, you will notice that the director wears many hats and has many duties. Often there are others to help with these tasks, but he or she must be prepared to take on the responsibilities regardless.

THE DIRECTOR IS A DRAMATURG: must understand the literary and historical background of the play, the author's background and intentions, the social climate of the times, and the style in which the play has been written (realism, farce, tragedy, and so on); must be able to explain the material to the actors and designers and place it in a context; must know how to do research in the library and Internet for all the information necessary.

THE DIRECTOR IS AN INTERPRETER: must be able to understand the deepest meaning of the play and what the playwright is saying about the world and then be able to explain it to the cast and staff of the production. This doesn't happen right away; often the meanings within the play don't reveal themselves until the director has been working for a while. Good plays have many layers.

THE DIRECTOR IS A CONCEPTUALIZER: must create the world of the play—its colors, images, moods, energies, shapes, and sounds—and decide whether to set it in the original setting or in a different time and place.

THE DIRECTOR IS A STAGER: must plan how to bring the play to life on the stage, moving bodies and creating the stage pictures that will best tell the story.

THE DIRECTOR IS AN ACTING COACH: must know how to work with and guide the actors—be able to express what is required and help them discover their characters and understand the play; must be patient and helpful with their memorizing and help to bring forth the best performances possible from them, despite inexperience, stage fright, or other problems.

THE DIRECTOR IS A CASTING DIRECTOR: must select the best person for the part, holding an audition that will bring each actor's potential to light and matching the actor with the character according to his or her interpretation of the play.

THE DIRECTOR IS AN ORGANIZER: must plan time well; must plan rehearsals to get the most out of the allotted time and be efficient and clear at meetings.

THE DIRECTOR IS A BUSINESS MANAGER: must ensure that everyone is staying within the budget, that the publicity is out and the tickets are printed, that the house manager is aware of dates and volunteers, and that royalties are paid.

THE DIRECTOR IS AN ART AND MUSIC CONSULTANT: must talk to designers about the set, music, lights, and costumes and must know about color, shape, and design elements; musical styles and sound effects; and other aesthetic elements for the play.

THE DIRECTOR IS A COUNSELOR: must be able to understand and talk to the cast about problems and fears and get inside the minds and hearts of the characters as well as the actors who portray them. Many things will come up during the rehearsals, and tact, patience, and good intentions are really put to the test.

THE DIRECTOR IS A COMMUNICATOR: must be able to talk clearly, verbalize ideas, find language to express thoughts and ideas that are hard to put into words, and assume a leadership role in discussions. Sometimes the director will have to justify and explain his or her artistic decisions (such as why the sky is red and not blue).

THE DIRECTOR IS A DELEGATOR: must be able to let others do the work they are meant to do, give some tasks to those who might do a better job, and ask for help. The director doesn't have to know how to hang the lights or sew the costumes but should know how to find the right person to do the job and allow him or her the opportunity to shine. As we have said, there is a place in theater for every talent. The director must assist in making all group members feel valued as they work together to make the magic happen.

YOUR THEATER GROUP

As you begin, pay attention to the group for whom you will be working. Is it a school theater group or drama club? Is it a local theater company? What type of play seems best for the company and for the time of year? Will it be a light, romantic comedy that works well in the spring? A Christmas show? A summer musical? Does the company have certain guidelines or restrictions? Is the material suitable for the age of the actors and the expectations of the company? Some groups like to do only musicals. Some like to do the work of new playwrights exclusively. Some companies prefer the classics or Shakespeare. Find out from the producers what type of scripts are best and what they expect.

Learn what the stage looks like, so that as you begin to plan your production you will understand the space and the limitations. Understand the budget guidelines.

Make sure you consider the amount of time you will have to plan and rehearse, what support staff you will have, and how many actors might show up for the audition.

If you are just handed a play to direct, decide if you really like it or could learn to like it. Will it be a learning experience and a good challenge to do the play or will it be a chore? These are considerations that affect everyone involved, because if you don't like the play, no one will enjoy the process.

YOUR AUDIENCE

Pay close attention to the audience you expect to have for your show.

- Is your audience mature or do you expect families with young children?

- Is your audience high school age?

- Is your audience bilingual and culturally diverse or homogeneous?

- Is your target audience specific, or do you expect a full range of ages and backgrounds?

Take all this into account as you work with your producer in choosing your show, and take into account the language and themes within the script.

Be sure you advertise something about the subject matter of the play. If the audience comes in expecting a light comedy and discovers the play is about something very violent, sexual, or scary, they will be unprepared and disappointed or, even worse, angry.

The wonderful part is that the audience will always meet you halfway even if there are flaws and a few mistakes here and there. I remember going to my daughter's high school production of *Inherit the Wind* years ago. They were doing fine when suddenly the scenery completely collapsed and fell over, right on top of two actors. One member of the cast just calmly hoisted the fallen wall back up, and they went right on with the play. The audience stood up and cheered!

The audience has been eagerly waiting for the show to go on. They have paid their money and are excited to see what is offered. Generally, they are quietly (or noisily) rooting for you and want things to be great. And without the audience, there is no show—just endless rehearsals!

STEP 2

THE CHANGING ROLES OF THE DIRECTOR

Direct: from the Latin word dirigere: *"To arrange in distinct lines" . . . therefore, to straighten or guide.*

THE DICTIONARY OF WORD ORIGINS

For the theatre as we understand it today three things are necessary: actors speaking or singing independently of the unison chorus; an element of conflict conveyed in dialogue; and an audience emotionally involved in the action but not taking part in it. Without these essential elements there may be religious or social ceremonies, but not theatre.

PHYLLIS HARTNOLL, THE THEATRE: A CONCISE HISTORY

I think it is vital to learn about the history of directing before you get started with an actual production. We need to know how the art of the theater developed to find our own place within it. Until the late 1800s, the term *director* was not really used. Modern directors have been working in new ways and with great freedom to be creative and to be in complete control of the entire artistic vision of a production. But what occurred previously? The following is a brief history of how theater began and who was in charge.

RITUALS

Our oldest forms of theater are rituals. Rituals use song, dance, or drama to connect the tribe or group with the gods, nature, or special events outside daily life, such as war, birth, death, marriage, or coming of age. Initially, rituals were forms of prayer done by the entire tribe. Then, as certain members of the tribe learned and performed more expertly, the rituals became more specialized, with leaders, choruses, and eventually spectators.

A ritual is a repeated, learned, and remembered pattern that communicates our deepest desires and fears to a higher power. Regardless of the differences between religions, countries, and people, every society on earth has its rituals. The coming-of-age rituals of bar mitzvah, quinceanera, and confirmation are well known. So are rituals for baptisms, marriage ceremonies, secret societies, fraternities and sororities, sporting events, and funerals. A ritual seeks to express hope and foster harmony and peaceful coexistence between humanity and nature and God. It is a shield against chaos and a plea for prosperity and order.

As rituals became more complex, tribal leaders were asked to oversee the performances. Thus, shamans, priests, rabbis, mullahs, teachers, or skilled singers or dancers would take the lead and set the ritual into place. Spiritual and ethical concerns would be enacted, and the entire tribe would be uplifted.

In the modern theater, rituals have been incorporated into many plays to connect the material to higher purposes. *God's Country* by Steven Dietz is a harrowing play that sheds light on and then indicts the Aryan Nations in America. Within the play are rituals for joining the brotherhood of a white supremacy group. In *Indians* by Arthur Kopit, the sacred Native American sun dance ritual is reproduced onstage. In both plays, these ritual reenactments strengthen our understanding of the connection between rituals and the deepest desires of those performing them.

THESPIS

We often hear the term *thespian* when people refer to actors or those who work in the theater. The word derives from the playwright and performer Thespis of Icaria. He traveled the known world of Greece and the neighboring city-states in a wagon as a storyteller, performing his original poems and dramas in approximately 534 BC. Although very little is known about him, he is credited to be the first man to win the playwriting prize in the annual festival to Dionysus and the first actor to step onto the stage as a solo performer in a drama, differentiated from the chorus.

GREEK THEATER

The Greeks honored their gods each year in a festival held in honor of Dionysus, son of Zeus, the god of fertility, prosperity, and wine. This festival was the most highly valued. Playwrights wrote tragedies, comedies, or comic interludes to honor Dionysus and to promote well-being within the community. The theater, itself, was called the City Dionysus. Tragedy in Greek means "goat song," and it is believed that either the prize for the winning tragedy was a goat or a goat was sacrificed in a ritualized celebration.

In Athens, Greece, in the fifth century BC, theater was alive and well. The playwrights Aeschylus, Sophocles, and Euripides were most revered, and their plays were staged annually for thousands of spectators at the City Dionysus. The language was poetic and elegant, and the themes were lofty and conveyed serious messages about ethics and morality.

An *archon*, or civil magistrate, selected the chorus, which was made up of wealthy citizens of the Athenian community. A *choregus* was appointed to each playwright, and he paid for the training and costuming of the chorus members and the musicians. Trained actors or soloists performed the leading roles. The *didaskalos* instructed the actors in the complex entrances and exits and the dances and songs. These three—the *archon*, the *choregus*, and the *didaskalos*—staged the productions.

Greek audiences were well educated and loved the annual playwriting contests. They were orderly and enthusiastic but never violent or unruly. Violent behavior was punishable by death!

At this time, as in all periods of history, there were also many traveling players, mimes, musicians, poets, and storytellers whose performances reflected daily life.

ROMAN THEATER

During the Roman era, comedies prevailed and shared popularity with large and lavish productions that featured enactments of sea battles (*naumachia*) staged on flooded amphitheaters or nearby lakes, gladiatorial contests, bear-baitings, fire-eaters, trapeze artists, and many more raucous and circuslike attractions.

State theater festivals were under the direction of managers, or *domini*, who contracted with city officials to perform at seasonal festivals. Actors were called *histriones*. In the first century BC, star performers were beginning to emerge. They were esteemed and wealthy citizens, well rewarded and treated as royalty.

THEATER FROM 1400 TO 1800

The increasing influence of Christianity in the second, third, and fourth centuries AD changed theater radically. Church councils threatened to excommunicate people who went to the theater. However, theater in the church was allowed, and many plays with biblical themes or tales of morality or of the crucifixion (mystery plays) were written, usually anonymously and performed inside the churches or church courtyards. Many scenes depicted heaven, purgatory, or hell with devils, fire-breathing monsters, and more. Such settings were staged on platforms called *mansions*. The mansions held scenery and props, and some were very elaborate.

The person in charge of all this was called the *conductor of secrets*, for the mansions held many props, smoke pots, and other seemingly magical illusions. The actors were well-meaning amateurs or, in England, members of a guild, similar to the trade unions of today. There was also the *pageant master*, who was a combination of a producer, stage manager, and, sometimes, actor. Often he would stay onstage through the whole show, helping with scenery or whispering forgotten lines to the actors.

THE ACTOR-MANAGER

Although there were enormous changes in government, religion, and society throughout the Renaissance, Restoration, and into the 1800s in Europe, little changed for the director of a theater company. Stages moved from churches to outdoor platforms to royal courts to lavish halls and theaters.

Traveling troupes flourished. The scenic arts changed and evolved, in particular developing perspective in set design Many different forms of theater and theater architecture developed, but the director was always known as the *actor-manager*.

Actors usually performed facing the audience directly when speaking or formed a semicircle and then moved upstage when their parts were concluded. Costumes were inconsistent; actors often wore the finest clothes they owned or outfits they liked. Little effort was made to accurately reflect the time period of the play.

The actor-manager's job was to coach the actors, deal with all the technical aspects, and, much of the time, the business aspects. And often he was a playwright and actor himself.

THE DUKE OF SAXE-MEININGEN, 1874–1890

Duke Georg II of Saxe-Meiningen, Germany, was a wealthy nobleman who loved theater and formed his own company of actors. They toured and performed all over Europe and Russia, and under his direction, the troupe become the most innovative company to ever produce and stage classical and modern dramas. His work inspired generations to come.

He became the first modern director. His first production was Shakespeare's *Julius Caesar*, and it was hailed as a masterpiece in which star performers and ensemble actors worked together effortlessly. His productions attempted realistic portrayals of characters and settings, accurate costuming, and a sense of perspective and balance on the stage. He rehearsed the actors intensely and was very precise about all the details of his shows.

Much has been written about his work, and the modern directors of the Moscow Art Theatre, the American Theatre Guild, the Free Theatre of France, and many more owe him much of the credit for defining the modern director as one who unifies a production and honors the playwright's intentions.

MODERN DIRECTORS

Modern directors have been freed up to concentrate on interpreting the script. Most agree that their primary job is to honor the playwright. That is done through working with the dramaturg, the designers, the actors—the whole ensemble. Their job is complete when the opening night curtain goes up. They are the visionaries who have created the world that the audience sees. They have worked hard for weeks or months until opening night, and then others in the company have the main responsibilities to continue presenting the show accurately. Modern directors do not have to prompt lines or fix costumes. They have the use of technology never known in previous centuries. Film, special effects, DVDs and CDs, slides and photographs—all sorts of mixed media can be brought onto the stage.

So the modern director is much freer than in the past; free to interpret the script in the best possible way.

NON-WESTERN THEATER

We tend to think of theater primarily as words played out on a stage, but in Africa, India, and Asia, theater has always been a blend of dance, music, and story, often simply referred to as "performance."

There are two categories of non-Western theater: classical and contemporary. Japan, China, India, and other Asian countries and the African nations have a rich heritage in both the classical and contemporary styles.

Classical theater harks back to traditional forms and strict training in formalized modes of performance. These usually reflect on timeless themes and have stood the test of many centuries. The training is long and hard, and the traditions are handed down from the elders over many years. Classical theater usually blends song, music, dance, and story. The function of the director in classical theater harkens back to the earlier style of actor-manager with the added job of teacher as well: one who instructs the younger performers on the correct methods for performing with beauty and accuracy.

Contemporary theater is about the modern world in which we live. These plays speak to the political and personal life in its current, social setting. Directors who work with contemporary themes approach the material in the same manner as European and American directors, and many have begun to blend non-Western styles with Western drama to create powerful and subtle productions.

You will be richly rewarded if you study the many performance styles of India, China, Japan, Bali, the African nations, and Latin America. The stories that are enacted, the uses of dance and music, and the staging techniques are inspiring and open our eyes to the wondrous variety theater has to offer.

STEP 3

How to Read, Understand, and Analyze a Play

A human being is the best plot there is!

JOHN GALSWORTHY, PLAYWRIGHT

In each play of any consequence you will find two powers locked in combat . . . conflict, therefore, is the quintessential of good playwriting, just as it is one of the inescapable conditions of life itself.

MICHAEL CHEKHOV, ACTOR, DIRECTOR, TEACHER

HOW TO READ A PLAY

Reading a play can be a tiresome chore. Sometimes we read a play because we have to: The play is an assignment in a class, or we know we're going to see the play or a film based on it and we want to familiarize ourselves with the words and story ahead of time. Plays are often the least appreciated form of literature, but they can be doorways into many complex and exciting stories that deal with the human condition.

The first thing to acknowledge is that the play is on the page, not on the stage. You must use your imagination, and how well you use it will determine how much you enjoy reading the play and how well you analyze and understand the deepest meanings that the author intended.

We most often read fiction, and we are used to the format of fiction writing, but there are a lot of differences between fiction and plays. It helps to look at some of those differences.

Fiction

1. Often there is a narrator—a first-person voice or an omniscient voice that sees and knows all.

2. The characters are direct to the reader—not filtered through an actor.

3. Words describe everything, including nature, weather, emotions, and private thoughts.

4. The movements are described or narrated: "She pointed to the baby and smiled."

5. The audience is one person—the reader.

6. It often takes a rather lengthy time to read a work of fiction.

Plays

1. The characters speak directly without "he said, she said."

2. The actors are playing the characters.

3. Description is only through the characters' words or the set as seen on the stage.

4. We see all the movements and gestures.

5. The audience is a group of people.

6. The play is usually completed in a brief amount of time (one to two hours).

THE FIRST READING

I have chosen a short play, *The Rising of the Moon* by the Irish playwright Lady Augusta Gregory, to demonstrate the key things to notice when reading a play (see Appendix for the play along with commentary on the play and a biography of Lady Gregory). I chose it for several reasons. It is short; you can read it quickly and then read it again. It has only a few characters. The setting is unusual and the language a bit difficult. It also has a definite mood, style, and arc of action, and it contains interesting moral questions.

To begin, just read through the play. Read it once, and if there are words or passages you don't understand, just keep going. You may want to highlight those words for later discussion or research.

A question that comes up often is: Do I read the italics (the stage directions and settings) or skip over them? The answer is: Yes, read them! They are an important part of the whole play. Read every word. If italics have been used in the play by the playwright, they are there to clarify the action and make things more vivid. They often describe the physical action that cannot be expressed in the dialogue and tell the reader about a character's physical qualities or his or her gestures or moods. They also describe the setting and the sounds that we are being asked to imagine.

Don't give up if you get confused by the characters or by something in the story. This is not an easy play, but keep going until you have finished.

After the First Reading

Ask yourself, or discuss with others, the following questions:

- Did I understand the story? What is the story? What happens?

- Did I understand the characters? Who are they?
- What do I believe the author was trying to tell me?
- What specific details did I notice about the play?
- What didn't I understand?
- What words or references were in the play?
- Did I enjoy the play?
- If yes, what made it enjoyable? If not, why not?

As a casual reader, you might stop here and not even bother to answer the questions. But, as a young theater director, actor, or stage designer, you must know how to interpret the material.

Before the Second Reading

There are certain things to consider so that you can fully grasp the meaning of the play. You can begin with any of the topics below because each one will open a door to all the others and then to the deepest meaning of the play, which we call the *spine*.

PLOT

The *plot* of a play is simply the story, "what happens." Not *how* it happens but *what* is the basic story.

It has a beginning, a middle, and an end. Sometimes a longer play will have two or three plots going on at the same time, sometimes weaving through each other. A plot line of a play usually follows a clear pattern:

1. THRESHOLD: The very beginning of the play; as you enter the story.

2. POINT OF ATTACK: The first hint of a conflict or complication.

3. COMPLICATIONS: Things that create conflict or trouble along the way. There can be many. The story builds one on top of another.

4. REVERSALS: Changes from the ongoing pattern. Often things are filled with conflict and then something peaceful occurs for a brief time: that is a reversal. Suddenly everything seems fine, then another complication makes it even worse.

5. CLIMAX: The highest point of dramatic significance in the play.

6. DENOUEMENT: Meaning "falling action," as the play moves toward its conclusion.

7. CONCLUSION: The ending. The way it ends is the way the author wants you to feel about the whole story.

SETTING, TOPOCOSM, VISUALS

The *setting* is the location of the story. In *The Rising of the Moon*, it is a wharf on the water in a small village.

The *topocosm* is the geographic locale where it occurs: in this case the seacoast of Ireland. Once you narrow the topocosm down to a specific place, it is easier to visualize the mood, colors, and setting that the author has put into the story. Plays do not describe things the way novels and poetry do. The description is implied by the setting and by symbols put in the play to express the meaning.

The *visuals* are everything that the audience sees: the set, lights, colors, scenery, props, costumes—the whole look of the play.

An important question to ask as you start the second reading is: How does the setting help lead you to the meaning of the play? Are there symbols used in the setting that explain the meaning?

MOOD

Mood is best described as the general feeling created by the words, the setting, the movements of the characters, and the music, lights, and colors used. Silences, shadows, and sound effects all contribute to creating a mood, and that mood might be upbeat or it might be grim. How does the mood lead you to the meaning of the play?

CHARACTERS

The characters form the heart of a play. If you have characters, you have story and action. And theater is always about characters in the grip of conflict. The main character of a play is called the *protagonist*, and the main person in conflict with the protagonist is the *antagonist*. Both words come from the word *agon*, which in Greek means "the struggle." The protagonist is for the struggle (or one who struggles with the conflict and ultimately the truth). The antagonist is the character who works against the struggle for the truth.

There are four basic ways to understand the nature of each of the characters.

1. What the character says (or doesn't say) in the text.

2. What the character does (or doesn't do).

3. What the character looks like, including age and health (as the writer informs you, or as you imagine).

4. What other characters say about him or her.

When thinking about these four ways, do you get a sense of what the characters want and don't want? What do their actions tell us? What do they fear? What do they believe in? Do you get a sense of their histories of past situations? Their secrets? How do the characters lead you to the meaning of the play?

CONFLICTS

There are five basic categories of conflict. One of the five will appear in every play and be the center of the problem. There may be other conflicts in the play as well.

1. A character in conflict with another character (person versus person)

2. A character in conflict with nature (the sea, Mt. Everest, Godzilla, and so on)

3. A character in conflict with God (or Fate or the super-natural)

4. A character in conflict with society (usually a corrupt or rigid society or an opposing group)

5. A character in conflict with himself (a personal struggle)

Which conflicts are at work in the play, and how does the awareness of these conflicts lead to the meaning?

LANGUAGE, DICTION, VOCABULARY

Every play will have specific *language* to tell the story, set the tone and the rhythms, and generally do the work of communicating what the author intends.

The language used in the play; in *The Rising of the Moon*, it's English.

Diction is a particular way of using language and rhythm. In this play, it is the diction of rural Ireland.

The *vocabulary* is particular to the characters and may include words you are not familiar with or don't understand. My suggestion is to not let a word here or there throw you off from the main work of the play. Keep reading and research word meanings later.

Reading aloud is a good habit to get into. The language has rhythms and idioms that will be a lot clearer to you if you read aloud. If you stumble over a word or two, just make a note of them.

Each character has his own way of speaking. Either the pitch, rhythms, nasality, tempo, or traits like pausing, stuttering, saying "you know" or "like" or other such habits make each person different. Our speech patterns make us who we are, and this is an important way of defining a character in a play. How do you imagine the characters in this play speak?

EMOTIONAL RANGE/AESTHETIC DISTANCE

EMOTIONS: Notice the use of emotions. Take note of them as you read through the next time. There are the explicit emotions that the characters are experiencing and expressing. And then there are the emotions that hide below the surface that the characters may be feeling but can't express. How do the various emotions change throughout the play? How do emotions lead you to the meaning of the play?

AESTHETIC DISTANCE: This is the emotional distance between the audience and the play. How close does the playwright let you come as you are trying to understand the character? Are you kept far away or are you let into the character's private world so that you are able to really care about him or her?

If the aesthetic distance is quite short, you have empathy (close connection) or sympathy (feeling of pity) for the characters. If it is quite a long distance, you may not feel much for the characters but simply see their behavior as telling a tale or delivering a moral lesson.

MUSIC, SOUND/SOUND EFFECTS, SILENCE

The use of sound is crucial to a play. The sound includes not just the words we read or see performed but the other noises found in the world of the play.

MUSIC: What music is suggested by the playwright? In the case of *The Rising of the Moon*, folk songs are woven into the script. As you research this play, you'll find that the title is from a revolutionary Irish ballad called "The Rising of the Moon." Obviously, there is a reason why music plays an integral part in the play.

What other music do you hear? Does the play itself suggest additional music that might also be used? This would be a director's choice, since the playwright has included what seems appropriate to the story and nothing more.

SOUND/SOUND EFFECTS: In the case of this play, do you hear other sounds? The sea? Foghorns? A dog barking? Think about what you might also hear in this situation. Will it add to the play or detract?

SILENCE: Silence can be a very powerful element in a play. It can create tension or feelings of awkwardness, mystery, or romance. If you choose to use silence instead of music, it may create an eerie or suspenseful effect. Use silence as an experiment and see what it creates in your work. In reading a play, imagine silences interjected between lines or between sections of the piece and notice how it makes you feel.

GENRE, STYLE, VERISIMILITUDE

GENRE: *Genre* defines the type of play. There are basically four kinds: comedy, tragedy, melodrama, and farce with many crossovers and subcategories.

Comedy was, originally, a play that did not have a tragic ending. Comedy is usually funny, but there are many kinds: comedy of wit or high comedy, in which the language is clever and makes us laugh because of its cleverness; comedy of manners; middle comedy, which satirizes the customs and artificial manners of a particular group; and comedy of life, in which the daily situations of our lives are looked at humorously. Usually, comedy points out the foibles and mistakes of our lives so we can laugh at them. Comedy avoids serious suffering. When there is suffering, we know it won't cause permanent damage or death; therefore, we can relax and laugh. If we feel serious worry or sadness, comedy disappears.

Tragedy is a play that is serious and evokes strong emotions in the reader or audience. Those emotions are usually pity, sympathy, or fear. Tragic plays end with death or disaster brought about by the central character who at some point in the drama comes to understand his or her own flaws and has a strong realization before the end.

Melodrama is a blend of tragedy and comedy. Some parts evoke sadness, others cause laughter. Usually good and evil are clearly defined. Melodrama can include musical interludes, romance, and violence interwoven with the main story.

Farce (low comedy) takes comedy to extremes with exaggerated physical activity and exaggerated characters with larger-than-life reactions.

STYLE: *Style* is the way reality is expressed in a play. There are many different styles, but the ones listed below are most often seen in theater.

Realism: an attempt to portray the world as directly as possible, not idealized or imagined. It shows things as they appear to the impartial eye of the beholder.

Naturalism: an attempt to portray life in its utmost reality, up close and often gritty. It shows the sights and sounds and smells of life with all its natural functions.

Expressionism: the grotesque parts of life. It moves away from realism and shows the inner world of the character with his or her distortions and terrors. The play usually follows the leading character and shows the world through his or her perspective. Exaggeration and extremes are shown.

Dadaism: an off-shoot of expressionism—disharmony and rebellion shown through broken or unrecognizable language (babble) or things out of the usual time sequences. It also includes calculated madness, collages, and unrelated situations.

Surrealism: a theater style that began in France between the two world wars that tries to show a fantasy world, dreams, and the subconscious mind at work and often leaves the interpretation to the audience.

Absurdism: a style that attempts to portray a search for meaning in a godless, chaotic world. It arose after World War II and tried to portray the effects of the horrors of that war. It didn't tell stories, but showed a world that was hopeless, boring, and meaningless. Characters were isolated from each other and often had unhealed wounds, both physical and emotional.

Classicism: a style based on formal lines, according to rules set down in the classical Greek and Roman periods. Plays are based on rational, logical principles of balance and symmetry and on moral and ethical ideas.

Romanticism: often thought of as the opposite of classical. It turns away from formal, rational ideas and embraces the mystical, the spontaneous, and highly individual themes. These romantic ideals may include the power of nature, the mysteries of life, and the inner, isolated spirit of humanity as opposed to humanity in a larger, structured society.

In what style do you think *The Rising of the Moon* was written?

VERISIMILITUDE: *Verisimilitude* is the believability of a play, whatever style the writer has chosen. This term is used to define the reality of the play. It is not enough to say a play is realistic; it might not be written in a realistic style, but rather in a surrealistic or absurdist style. Verisimilitude means the truth of the play and its setting and characters regardless of which style has been chosen to portray it.

STRUCTURE

Notice how the play is set up. Short plays usually have a clear beginning, middle, and climax, followed by a quick ending. Longer plays can be analyzed by noting when a scene begins and ends and how the scenes are built to add more and more conflict.

MEANING, SPINE

All the previous work leads to this: What is the *meaning* of the play? Your work as a director (or informed reader) is to identify the themes and ideas of the play.

- What is Lady Gregory's main thought in the work?
- With whom do you identify and who expresses the main thoughts?

- Who is the protagonist? Is he a hero?
- What are the conflicts?
- Where is the climax?
- How is the play resolved?

The *spine* is the main idea that supports the whole play. It should be a simple thought in one sentence. Can you state what the spine is in this play?

THE SECOND READING

Keeping all the foregoing in mind, read the play again. During the second reading, you should be able to really understand the material if you go through all the points mentioned.

Usually your first impressions will lead to a sort of subconscious understanding of the play. Start there. Start, also, with one thing you know for sure in the text and open your thinking out from there.

Now is the time to do additional research, looking up words you don't know. Words you may want to look up are *assizes*, *pastepot*, *placard*, *peeler*, *pike*, *Granuaile*, and *vale*.

ANALYSIS OF *THE RISING OF THE MOON*

The first thing to look at is the setting, written in italics. It is nighttime and the moon is shining. It is a seaport town, not a big city. The wharf is deserted. There are stairs going down to the water. No boat. It does not reveal what time of the year it is. There are posts and chains and a big barrel (big enough for two men to sit on comfortably and smoke). If there is a breeze, we would hear the chains rattle a bit and the posts creak. The sound of the ocean is always present. Since we do not know the weather condition, the director might make it windy or calm.

The opening line of the play reveals a great deal. Many plays tell you about the theme and meaning in the very first line. In Shakespeare's *Hamlet*, the guard says: "Who's there?" And that is the whole question that Hamlet deals with throughout the play. The play asks: Who am I? What should I do to fulfill my destiny? What is my life all about?

In *Romeo and Juliet*, the prologue states: "Two households, both alike in dignity," and that statement tells us, immediately, that good and bad are not the questions here. The tragedy will occur without having polarized positions, and we will have to look at bigger issues in which both families have our sympathy and pity.

The opening line of this play, spoken by Policeman B, is: "I think this would be a good place to put up a notice" (and he points to the barrel). We know immediately that the barrel will be of importance: It will display a wanted poster, and that is the whole story of this play. A man is wanted, and the police are sent to find him. When the Sergeant and the Ragged Man sit together on the barrel, the whole story shifts, so it is a "good" place, but not in the way we first are led to believe. Also, the word *notice* has two distinct meanings here: a wanted poster and the verb "to notice," which the Sergeant ultimately does—takes notice of his own life and what he believes to be the better choice.

The first few lines of the play also tell us a lot. The two policemen ask the Sergeant (who is older and their superior officer) about putting up the poster, but he doesn't answer right away. In a short play, where there are only a few pages, why does the playwright take up half a page telling us that the Sergeant doesn't reply? He is distracted and is looking down the stairwell. That tells us he has troubling thoughts about the situation right from the beginning. When he finally speaks, he tells us a lot of important information—about where the stairs lead and what he fears might happen. He is preoccupied with that thought.

Remember: we know about characters by what they say and what they *do not* say, so the Sergeant's silences tell us a great deal about his distracted reply. This is the *point of attack* in the play; the first moment where we sense a conflict.

Then there is the discussion about the reward, the man's physical appearance, and the conflict that the police face if he is caught. The government wants him caught. The people of the town do not. The police work for the government, but they are also local men. The conflicts continue.

Remember: We also know about a character by what *other people say* about him. So we find out, through the discussion, that he is small and dark and he has escaped from jail during the time of the assizes, in which the police feel there should have been better protection. The assizes was similar to a grand jury that met quarterly to judge criminal and civil cases. Here we have quite a bit of exposition before we ever meet him.

What is the structure of the play? How is it divided? The scenes are broken in several ways. If we divide the play by French scenes (see Step 6 for a further discussion of French scenes), which is a useful way to rehearse a play, we see there is a three-person scene, then a monologue, then a two-person scene, then a four-person scene with one character hiding behind the barrel (the audience may see him even though the policemen do not; if you were directing the play, that would be a choice you could make), then a two-person scene, and a final moment where the Sergeant does a concluding set of lines alone.

In each section, it will be useful to decide what the objective is for each character. What do they want? What circumstances add to or change the objectives?

The Sergeant wants the reward of 100 pounds. We find out he is a married man and of course can use the money. This is a major motivation for him and will be the turning point later.

The younger policemen want to do their jobs correctly and be "good cops." They want to rearrest this guy and be praised for their work.

What does the Ragged Man want? To escape. And what is he willing to do to get what he wants? Disguise himself as a ballad singer. But there is more here. The Ragged Man has a certain attitude: cocky, self-assured. But what's behind that? He believes he can fool the Sergeant and stays around to sing and smoke. But he is also a philosopher and a revolutionary and has put his life on the line for his political beliefs. He says things like "Life is precious," "You will get your reward in heaven." Only when he has achieved his goal of changing the Sergeant's heart and mind can he truly get away.

It is important to look at power in a play. Who has it in the beginning of the play? Who has it at the end? In this play the Sergeant has the power and retains it all the way through. You might be tempted to think the escaped revolutionary has the power at the end, but in truth, the Sergeant changes enough to become enlightened when he remembers his past and how his life might have been different. Thus, he allows the man to escape.

He sees the wisdom in the man's words and presence. He acknowledges: "I had a great spirit in those days." He never surrenders his power, but he uses his awareness for the good of the Ragged Man.

The barrel is a powerful symbol. It starts out as the place to slap on the wanted poster, then later it becomes the object that binds the two men together as well as a high vantage point to see what may be approaching from the sea. The Ragged Man, while they are talking and smoking, suggests what the Sergeant might have been if his life had turned out differently:

> And maybe one night, after you had been singing, if the other boys had told you some plan they had, some plan to free the country, you might have joined with them . . .

The barrel provides a solid platform for them. A meeting ground. A support.

The woman, Granuaile, was otherwise known as Grace O'Malley. If you do your research, you will find that she was the notorious and wonderful pirate queen of sixteenth-century Ireland (1530–1603) sometimes called the "Sea Queen of Connemara." To the Ragged Man, she is the symbol of pride, strength, and freedom and rebellion against the British crown.

Even today she represents the brave struggle against British rule. Her life inspired songs, stories, plays, and novels.

The songs take up a big space in the play. What purpose do they serve? Just to mention two of them: "The Peeler and the Goat" obviously is an unpopular one and nobody gets to hear it. The song of Shawn O'Farrell is about revolution, and the Sergeant doesn't want to hear it! Songs have always been a powerful part of any political movement. What part do they play in this story?

The *anagnorisis* is the moment of recognition after which everything changes. Certainly we can find this in the play. The Sergeant has a moment that is not written in the dialogue. As the man removes his wig, the Sergeant, shocked, says, "It's a pity. It's a pity!," and he repeats this again as the other policemen approach. At first he says, "I am in the force, . . . I will not let you pass," but then he allows the man to hide and, even though it isn't stated, to escape.

Pity is one of the most profound emotions we have. Aristotle says that pity and terror are the main emotions of serious drama. In comedy, these emotions do not occur, or if they do, we never take them as life threatening or final. We never really have to worry or fear in a comedy because the ending is filled with humor and relief.

The Sergeant says, "It's a pity," but what he really means is "I have pity for you." Pity implies that there is a feeling of compassion in a time of suffering that moves from the listener to the person who is suffering. Because he feels this, the Sergeant cannot remain the same. He has changed. He allows the man to hide until the others have left the wharf. His behavior demonstrates that he is a true hero: he is capable of change and can act for the good of others at his own expense (not getting the reward).

And the spine? If you could reduce the meaning of the play to one word, what would it be? Courage? Heroism? Compassion? Duty (to a higher calling)?

A play does not have one interpretation. This is just a suggested way to look at the text. You have options. As a young director, actor, or designer, you may want to look at other ways of working with this material. But remember there is a basic formula for analysis: plot, characters, music (and diction), spectacle, and meaning. To go back over these again:

- Always begin with the *plot*. Three policemen go to the wharf. They seek a wanted man. He appears to the Sergeant, and after time spent together, the Sergeant lets him slip away.

- Then move to *characters*. We have discussed them a bit, but you may want to create biographies for each of the men based on what the playwright has given us. What have the men been through? How do they look? What struggles show on their faces and in their bodies?

- Then move on to *music*. There is the music of the songs and the music of the language. Also, in this short play we have the music of the sea.

- There is *spectacle*. Consider everything visual.

- Lastly, *meaning*, which includes, symbols, themes, and spine. We have discussed some of this, but of course, there is always more to discuss. The play is rich and layered.

If you were to analyze the play, what other options or choices might you have?

STEP 4

THE FUNDAMENTALS OF DIRECTING

I can take any empty space and call it a bare stage. A man walks across this empty space whilst someone else is watching him, and this is all that is needed for an act of theatre to be engaged.

PETER BROOK, DIRECTOR

DEDICATION

Dedication is a fundamental factor in beginning your work as a director. Before you begin rehearsing a play, before you meet with your actors, your design team, and your crew, you must ask yourself: "Do I love this material?" I think it is not productive to work on a play you don't absolutely love. There are many plays out there and many to choose from, so the first basic premise is: *Love your material.*

Notice I didn't say "like" because I think it takes real strength to stay with a play over the hard times, the little mistakes, the big mistakes, and the many bumps in the road before opening night. Only love will carry you through! And please don't be afraid of the word *love.* A directing job engages you fully and completely. The script is with you morning and night. You have made a commitment to it and to the playwright. That is a passionate process. If you approach it as though you were going to the grocery store for dog food, it will show in your final product.

Now sometimes you are assigned a play to direct and you may not automatically like it. Other times, a producer may offer you a show and the rewards (either money or fame!) might be worthwhile and you take the show for that reason. But, you don't love the material. What do you do? I would say, *decide to love it*, and then begin to work on it. If you absolutely can't get into it and believe in it, decline the offer.

Most plays that have stood the test of time or are quite well known have something to offer. If you sign on as the director, it will be your job to find a reason to love the script before you begin. How do you do this? Well, you might really like the characters. They might be odd or funny or involved in situations that are important. You might respect the message. Perhaps the message of the play is very meaningful to you and says something about the world that you think will be valuable to share. Perhaps you like the style. Musical? Slapstick comedy? Serious drama? The style may be enough of a temptation to challenge you and convince you to work on it. Maybe you just love the setting or the period of history. Start with what you do love and go from there. I think you will find that it will be an interesting opportunity to stretch your ideas of what you enjoy.

CONCEPT

Once you find a reason to be excited about the material, you can begin to map out your concept of the play. This should be something you do alone, not in discussion with others. Working on *concept* is the true creative process for a director. We know that the job of the director is to interpret the material of the playwright not invent it. But your concept of how to work on the material is the creative part. Concept is the outward expression of how you feel about the play. It implies that you have found a way to show, through the style and manner of your interpretation, what the play means.

You can decide on the time period. You can decide on the look of the play, the style of the costumes and props. Will you set it in its original setting or update it? If you are working on a modern play, you are limited to what the living playwright requests, but if you are working on material from the ancient

Greeks to the nineteenth century, you may want to find a way to make it more relevant to modern audiences by setting it in our own time or in a period of history that would be similarly relevant. These plays are in the public domain, and therefore flexible interpretation is possible.

Then you must think about how you can reproduce your concept. That will be how you demonstrate your creativity. It will be a process of you finding ways to show us how you feel.

For example: If the sea in *The Rising of the Moon* seems very symbolic (to you) in the play because you see it as the means to freedom for the Ragged Man and ultimately freedom for the revolutionaries, you may want to emphasize the sound, colors, and feel of the sea. You could do this with sound and lighting effects. Remember, the meaning of the play is already in the material. You cannot rewrite the meaning, but your concept can bring it out, illustrate it, and emphasize certain key points.

You might wish to set the play in modern-day Ireland. Many of the same conflicts are still continuing. You might want to set it in the Ireland of the 1920s or before World War II. Concept doesn't have technique attached to it. There is not just one way: your creativity will be in finding the means to bring your interpretation alive.

As you proceed, be sure you can answer some basic questions:

- What will the technical needs in the play be?
- What function do the characters have in the play?
- Can my actors handle these roles?
- What will be the best way to stage this production?

BASIC STAGING

Once you begin working on the show, your biggest job will be to create the stage pictures that will tell the story. The placement of the actors and the movements that they make to create the action will be your biggest undertaking.

Moving your actors around the stage is called *blocking*. You will block the actors to walk, run, sit, and stand according to the situation in the script. Some playwrights tell you exactly what they want: "He walks to the barrel." Other playwrights do not tell you very much, and you must decide what the best move might be to get both the right action and right balance to the stage picture.

The picture you create with each arrangement of movements is called *picturization*. Blocking and picturization are both created by movement, and there are two major kinds of movement: stage movement and body movement.

Stage Movement

The stage is divided into three major planes and nine major zones. The three planes, horizontally formed, are:

- Downstage

- Centerstage

- Upstage

The zones are:

- Downstage left, center, and right

- Centerstage left, center, and right

- Upstage left, center, and right

On the next page, see the illustration of the zones of the stage. Notice when we say "stage left," it is the actor's left. All stage directions are from the point of view of the actor, so the director, sitting out in the audience, must think in reverse. When you call out, "Please walk two steps upstage right," you are actually having the actor walk to your left! This is called *audience left* because it is from the viewpoint of an audience member.

Each plane and each zone has a different emotional feeling to it. Being downstage makes the actor closer to the audience. It

Zones of the Stage

Upstage Right •	Upstage Center •	Upstage Left •
Centerstage Right •	Centerstage Center •	Centerstage Left •
Downstage Right •	Downstage Center •	Downstage Left •

can feel intimate or confrontational depending on the action. Being up close can create sympathy for the character or it can make us afraid of him. Being centerstage has a feeling of balance to it; it is in the middle and allows us to think about the character but not get too involved with her.

Being upstage has a feeling of distance, and that also has emotions around it. We can feel the solitude or remoteness of the character or we can feel a bit of mystery and unavailability. Diagonals create a sense of time and distance as well. Likewise, stage right, stage left, and centerstage have power.

Centerstage usually creates the feeling of balance, power, stability, and believability, but be careful about this because it can be boring to be balanced all the time. Asymmetry creates tension and conflict.

The other two areas have angles for your audience members' eyes, and you might want to experiment with these zones to see which angle gives you the feeling you want.

Don't be afraid to ask your actors to move from zone to zone until you get the effect you desire.

Body Movement

The body onstage has eight positions it can assume. Think of an actor turning in slow circles onstage, and he will hit all the positions eventually.

The most direct positions are full front and full back. They are bold and balanced. Each has its own power.

The quarter positions allow us to see the faces of the actors while they seem to be looking at each other.

The profile positions are very strong, but they exclude the audience from the subtle facial expressions and are more remote.

The three-quarter positions are quite mysterious and even more remote. We can only see a bit of each actor's face. You may or may not want that effect. It can create a sly feeling, a hidden feeling, or a shy feeling. It will also be useful in "giving" the scene to another actor so that the speaking actor has focus in a quarter position and the other actor, in three-quarter, does not have focus.

Body Positions

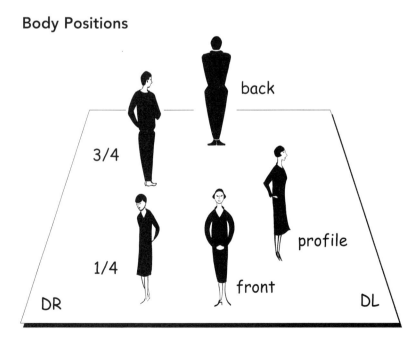

You may also subdivide the body angles, so that an actor's body is facing profile right, but he is looking over his shoulder quarter left. This creates interesting patterns, and the director can certainly ask his or her actor for combinations of angles.

Blocking

The most important part of staging your play is blocking—when you plan all the movements the actors will make during the play. It is the hard part of the rehearsal process, but once it's complete, you have the entire "dance" of the show. Blocking includes:

- Exits and entrances
- Crosses
- Sharing, giving, and taking scenes using the parts of the stage and the angles of the body
- Balancing the stage in relation to the set (walls, doorways) and the set pieces (furniture)
- Giving focus to the proper actor at the proper time

As you start to block your show, don't be afraid to try different paths and patterns: "Should she walk stage right and sit down? No . . . Let's try walking stage left and sitting on the floor." Keep experimenting until you get what you like, then write it down. Your job as a director is to block your actors effectively so they can be seen and heard at all the necessary times. You must consider:

- PROPER PLACEMENT: Actors are appropriately placed for what is needed in the scene.
- EMPHASIS: The audience members' eyes should be directed to the proper place so that the actor has focus.
- MOTIVATION: Movement must have a reason. As humans, we move all the time, but there is always a reason. We

need to move, have to move, want to move. As the director, you must help the actor find the reason for moving.

How do we achieve these goals? First, allow the script to do most of your work for you. The material, as written, will have specific guidelines. If not, trust your instincts. Would the character stand up and pace around while saying her lines? If it feels right, try it out. You can always change it later if it doesn't work.

Next, remember that you want to keep the audience focused on what is important. Don't get a messy, overcrowded stage. We won't be able to find the important character. Try the different parts of the stage until you have placed the actors in just the right location for the right emphasis.

Let's look at the basics of blocking.

CROSS: A cross occurs when an actor moves from one point to another. It can be in a straight path or a curved path. The curved path is used to avoid furniture or another actor, to be more visible to the audience, or to take up time as your actor speaks lines.

COUNTERCROSS: In a two-person situation, Actor A moves stage left (or right) and Actor B moves into Actor A's space (but a little upstage) to balance things off or "counter" (see illustration for countercross on next page).

SHARING: Two actors are in symmetrical or balanced positions. They have equal focus and equal audience attention.

DRESSING THE STAGE: This blocking spreads out the actors on the available stage space. Sometimes when actors go all the way to the edges of down right and down left, it is called "tying down the stage." This helps create a more substantial, balanced picture.

BALANCE: You want the stage to be equally interesting on all sides. So think about the placement of bodies versus furniture; bodies versus bodies; bodies on levels; and bodies against walls.

Cross

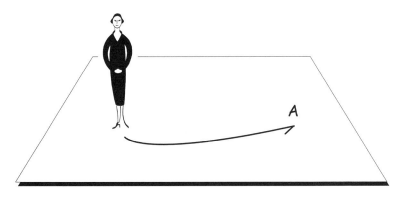

Countercross

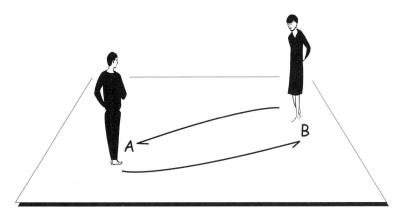

Sharing

in profile

in quarters

Levels

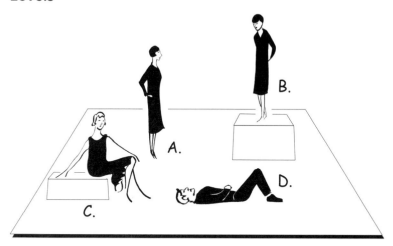

Never have your main actors diminished by big pieces of furniture. Make sure the actor who is speaking is in plain sight and never buried by other bodies. A crowd can be the same visual weight as one actor if the solo actor is a bit more downstage and has the focus through lines, light, or movement.

LEVELS: Levels can give you much visual excitement and create balance in unusual ways. Levels include trap doors, the floor, low stools, chairs, cubes, high stools, ladders, low platforms, risers, high platforms, scaffolds, and second floors. Experiment with levels to create visual patterns and focal points. Levels also create movement for the actors and the audience members' eyes. This makes things onstage far more engaging.

Exits, Entrances, Endings

Entrances are the hardest part of a play. The actor should have a clear path, clear motivation, and know where he has been and where he is entering.

- Entrances should be emphatic unless the actor is needing to sneak in unseen.

- Horizontal entrances are not as strong as diagonal entrances.

- Upstage entrances that move downstage are stronger.

- Entrances announce the beginning of a new French scene. (French scenes are determined by the entrance or exit of a character. This method of breaking down a play is discussed more fully in Step 6.)

- Exits announce a shift in energy and are the end of a French scene and the beginning of a new French scene.

- The ending of a scene should have a clear break through rhythm or tone of voice, music, or lights.

- The end of an act must also have conclusive action as well as a light shift, blackout, or something that tells the audience there will be a break, intermission, or bow.

Stage Business

Stage business is the smaller activities your actors do while saying their lines. Business can be in the script (imposed) or something you invent to make the scene more interesting and complete (implied).

- Imposed business is written in italics: *(She tied her shoes.)*

- Implied business is suggested by the director: "Let's have you tie your shoes as you tell him you love him."

Make sure you do not overburden your actor with too much business. If you see the actor is struggling, simplify.

Stage business sometimes requires extra props (cigarettes, cell phone, nail polish, bowl of snacks, drinks, and so on). Make sure you add any extra props to your prop list and be reasonable with your requests. If you include perishable food on the list, will there be someone to provide it and store it each night? Is it in the budget?

Stage business will draw the audience's attention in a scene. If you have a character in the background eating a big bowl of spaghetti, it will take the focus away from the main character who may be doing a monologue. Business for supporting characters should be performed in the correct proportion to the main character.

Business can help define a character. How he handles his cigarette tells us something about him. How she combs her hair can be revealing. The manner in which a prop is used is called an *endowment*. The actor endows the prop with the emotion he is feeling at the time.

Stage business creates a fuller, more entertaining realism to your scene and keeps it from becoming static, talky, or dull.

Specific Blocking Needs

The number of actors onstage create different visual and movement requirements. The basics will always be to:

- See and hear the actor
- Give focus to the appropriate person
- Be faithful to the action in each situation
- Create picturization that holds the audience's attention

As you block the play, check and respect your sight lines. The audience might not be able to see the areas on stage right and left due to the nature of the theater space.

MONOLOGUES AND SOLILOQUIES

Actor A

A monologue is a part of the play in which one actor speaks and no one interrupts. Usually the speech is at least ten or twelve lines, but it can go on for one, two, or several pages. There are some plays that are all monologues. In a monologue, the character is speaking to someone. It can be to:

- Herself or a part of herself

- God, life, fate, a ghost

- Her family, a friend, or an enemy

- An absent person whom she remembers and speaks to

- The audience or someone (or some group) onstage who is listening to her without responding in words (That person may respond with facial expressions or sounds, or even one or two words.)

If the character is performing a soliloquy, he is speaking to himself and revealing something about his inner thoughts or feelings. But essentially the actor is speaking in an unbroken sequence. Usually the speaking actor will face the audience or the other character(s).

A monologue is a revealing part of the play. It starts with something general and moves to a very personal, private place. This may be in the words or in the emotions behind the words. The character speaks to gain control or clarity about a circumstance. Every sentence usually supports a desire to state a conflict or resolve the conflict in some way.

Because the character speaks without interruption, there is usually no one to work against verbally. Therefore, the stage is essentially the solo actor's, and she can move almost anywhere to have the effect that is wanted. Centerstage is the most powerful. Higher levels are powerful.

Use contrast to create focus. Sitting in a chair when others are standing is powerful, and standing when everyone else is seated is also very powerful.

If others who are onstage look at the speaker, that gives the speaker the focus. If the speaker addresses the audience directly (presentationally), the closer to the downstage area he is, the stronger he will be.

Since the stage is essentially open for the monologue, experiment with different stagings: have the actor move around while he speaks then have him stay in one place and say the words with the proper emotions. Don't be tempted to "overdecorate." Sometimes, simply saying the lines and holding a strong place on the stage is your best bet.

Notice in *The Rising of the Moon* that the Sergeant has two short monologues. In the first he is speaking to Policeman B. In the second, on the same page, he only has three lines, but he has action. He walks up and down, once or twice, and looks at the placard. That physical activity can be very revealing and can replace words. He is alone onstage and has the space to himself to briefly reveal his personality. I call that a "physical monologue."

Later he has another short speech with the Ragged Man in which he addresses him directly, but he is speaking of important issues that move him toward a larger focus about what "might have been." Perhaps he starts out facing the policeman and then turns more full front, so the audience shares in the subtle emotions of the speech.

One-person scenes are fun. If no one else is onstage, the director and actor might collaborate on what feels best. The actor may have good ideas about what movements and what sort of timing works best. If there is a monologue with others present onstage, the director should concentrate on finding focus for the speaker and balance for the stage picture.

TWO-PERSON SCENES

Two-person scenes are the most frequent staging situations in theater. Certainly in *The Rising of the Moon*, the dialogue between the Sergeant and the Ragged Man form the heart and soul of the play. They are symbolic of the very root of drama, which, remember, is conflict.

In any play you read, one character essentially says yes the other says no, and there you have it! Or, one says, "I love you,"

Examples of Two-Person Scenes

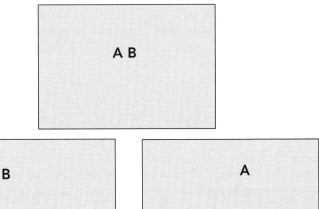

and the other says, "I love you, too," which starts out being peaceful and sweet, but rest assured, it won't last. Something will come along to create a conflict!

In staging two-person scenes, you have the possibilities of sharing as well as giving and taking. Sharing doesn't have to be in close proximity. One actor can be centerstage left and face profile right, while the other is centerstage right, facing profile left. They are at extreme opposite sides of the stage, looking at each other, and equal in their positioning.

- Decide who has the focus and who has the power in the scene.

- Decide on the movement plot. Do they walk around? Do they sit? Together? Opposite? Facing the audience? Do they embrace? Fight? Dance? Sit at a dinner table?

- In each situation, keep in mind who is speaking. Does that actor have clear focus? Will the audience pay attention to her? Does the other actor support the focus? If one is seated and the other is standing, who will be stronger?

- In close scenes, such as embracing, dancing, or fighting, make sure the actor who is speaking is visible to the audience and not buried in the shoulder of the nonspeaking actor. Try many different combinations of two-person arrangements as your actors go through their lines, and select the positions that are the strongest. Remember that we want to see and hear both actors at all times.

- One thing else to remember: The characters may not always have to look at each other. In fact, very often when we are talking to someone, we look elsewhere—at our feet, at the scenery, at others who pass by. At times we don't *want* to look at the other person for any number of reasons—shyness, anger, boredom, and so on. Decide whether the scene will be stronger if the characters avoid eye contact during certain moments.

THREE-PERSON SCENES

Three-person scenes are a different bag of tricks! There is a lot more going on than in a two-person scene, and only one more body has been added.

- There will be geometric designs created at every move of the scene. These designs are usually triangles, either symmetrical or odd angles. Three bodies in the space automatically create triangles unless they are in a straight line or a diagonal. Even with levels, you will see a triangulation.

- Straight lines are very dull onstage unless there is a good reason for them. Military drills, chorus-line dancers, police lineups—those work well! Otherwise, try to zigzag your three actors a bit so we keep interest in the visual picture.

Examples of Three-Person Scenes

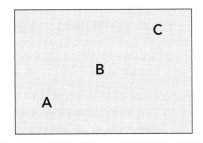

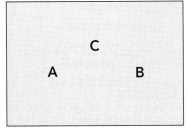 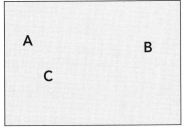

- Diagonals are good for a sense of perspective. The actor in the downstage position will be closest to us, most intimate and in the "now" moment of time. Further upstage, the appearance of the past becomes visual.

  For example, if you are showing three generations of men in a family and place the child downstage, the dad centerstage, and the grandfather upstage on a diagonal, you will give the illusion of time passing.

- Three-person scenes are often referred to as *tearing scenes.* One person is often caught between two conflicted characters, and the middle character is *torn* between them. As you stage your three-person scenes, think about the placement of the middle character. It can work symbolically to place her between the other two.

- There is also the two-against-one scene. Logically, placing the two who are in agreement together and the one who is opposed somewhat separated is equally symbolic. You may want to go with this, or try more daring arrangements!

- Be sure that each actor can be seen and heard. Keep all three actors alive in the scene even if they do not have equal focus. The audience will look at each character, even if he or she doesn't speak.

- Avoid chaos. Keep the paths of movement clear and simple, with the actor who speaks having the primary activities.

FOUR-PERSON SCENES

Many of the same rules apply to four-person scenes as do to three-person scenes.

- As always, you want everyone seen and heard.

- Avoid straight lines unless there is a purpose.

- Think of the strength of diagonals.

- Keep the pathways uncluttered and keep focus on the speaker through groupings, eye contact, and levels.

- Keep stage business unobtrusive.

- Around a dinner table, be sure the actors at the sides "cheat out" a bit so they can be seen fully. Usually the audience side of the table is left open.

- The danger that you run into with four-person scenes is static, symmetrical positioning. Keep bodies asymmetrical: three and one, two and one and one, and so on. Levels help. Try having two sit, one stand, one lean against something. Use your set to help explore visual interest in the bodies.

- After all this, you still may want to break some rules and try symmetry. It is very powerful and has many connotations: balance, dependability, stability, nobility, royalty, confidence. I once saw the Royal Household Dancers of

Examples of Four-Person Scenes

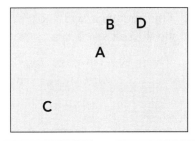

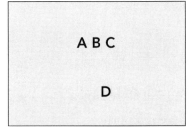

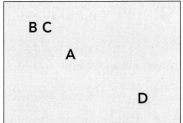

Japan perform. Four men moved very, very slowly in the four corners of a boxing ring for hours. They were perfectly symmetrical and it was amazing.

- In *The Rising of the Moon*, the four-person scene in the play has one man hiding. We have discussed the idea that the director should choose whether the audience sees the Ragged Man or not. If we see him, it is a four-man scene, with one character crouched down at a lower level, not making eye contact. This makes for interesting picturization.

GROUP SCENES

All the same rules apply.

- Avoid traffic jams and clutter.
- Direct the audience's attention to where you want it to go by using diagonals and levels.

- Stage right is a stronger area than stage left. Trust me, it just *is*. Theories are plentiful, but the strongest theory is that most audience members are right-handed and therefore the crossover to their left is easier on the eyes.

- Balance your stage. One strong speaker can hold off a huge crowd if he is downstage or on a riser or staircase and speaks clearly, facing the audience (even though he is addressing a crowd onstage.)

- Every actor in the crowd is important. Have a plan for each one. Have a traffic pattern and a set of character traits and movements.

- Using the house, the balconies, the aisles—the whole theater—can be a lot of fun and very powerful. You add the element of surprise, you increase your playing space, and you include the audience. But the audience must know where to look first, so the use of sound, and especially lighting, will help you create focus.

- Keep control. When you are rehearsing with a lot of actors, things can get rowdy, and it will be hard to concentrate. You may want to have some preliminary sketches of your ideas for the space before you come to rehearsal. But don't be afraid to make lots of changes and experiment a lot. And ask people to please understand that this is a rehearsal and you need to think!

We do not have a large group scene in *The Rising of the Moon*, but here's an example of how you might create one: What if, when the policemen returned, there were five of them instead of two? The wharf becomes very crowded. The Ragged Man is crouched behind the barrel. The actors are all speaking. Even if they don't have actual lines, you can bet they might be making sounds of some sort. It's cold, rainy, late: they may be shivering, huffing, maybe joking a bit. Of the five policemen and the Sergeant, who is most important? Who gets the focus? Where will you put him? He knows the Ragged Man is hiding. He

Example of a Group Scene

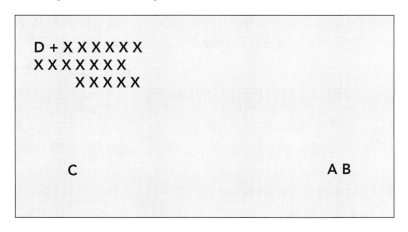

wants the others to leave. The others offer to stay, and then they eventually do go.

In a crowd scene, all the actors must strive to stay in character and think of business and small movements in keeping with the situation. The worst thing that can happen in a crowd scene (and often does) is that one actor will go flat, look totally bored, and you just know he's planning what to have for dinner after the show and is not staying in the scene. This takes away all the believability in the scene

Plan the traffic pattern. Plan the entrances and exits. Make sure everyone is seen and heard. Help the actors to know what they are looking at and where their eyes should focus. Lastly, don't be afraid of crowd scenes. Use common sense and follow the guidelines. You will have some exciting moments on your stage.

NOTES ABOUT RHYTHM, TEMPO, AND ARC

After your blocking is complete and you begin to stage your play, begin thinking about rhythm, tempo, and arc.

Rhythm

Rhythm is the basic heartbeat of your play. You have heard of "the rhythm of life," "the rhythm of the city," "the motor's rhythm." Rhythm moves your play along—a regularly reoccurring pattern of energy brought about by the dialogue and the action. It can be harsh or sweet, frightening or relaxing.

Tempo

The speed of your rhythm is the tempo. You have a song; let's say a rap song. The rhythm is set, but the tempo can go faster or slower. There are fast rap songs and slow, cool rap songs. The tempo in a play changes from beat to beat during the play. Some beats will require a slow speed, others go fast.

Arc

The arc is the line of the rhythm and tempo of your play. The arc charts the conflicts within the characters as the conflicts increase and develop, reach a climax, then subside and finally conclude at the ending.

WHAT THE ACTOR NEEDS TO DO

Stage Movement

The fundamentals of stage movement are basic concepts you learn as you study acting or as you start rehearsing a play. Your job is to remind or teach the actors the basic stage directions and body positions. Either in classes, or during a first rehearsal, go over and be clear about the parts of the stage and the angles of the body. Be sure you remember crosses and sharing (or not sharing) scenes.

Character Work

When you cast a show and assign the roles, your real work as a director begins. You and your actors will discuss the nature of the roles, and then it is the actor's job to work on developing the part. Some ways to do that are as follows.

WHAT THE CHARACTER SAYS

What words does the character use? What vocabulary? What regional accent?

What are the character's favorite words?

Does the character use a lot of jargon, curse words, or code words?

How fast or slow does the character speak?

What pitch is the voice? How loud or soft?

How often is the character silent?

How well does the character express what he or she means?

Does the character stutter? Lisp? Repeat filler words such as *umm, like, ya'know*?

Does the character stretch out his or her words and exaggerate sounds?

Does the character drop certain sounds such as the final g's (I'm goin')?

What topics does the character discuss? What topics are *never* discussed?

WHAT THE CHARACTER LOOKS LIKE AND DOES

What type of body? Thin? Fat? Tall? Short?

What sort of posture? Stiff? Flexible? Graceful? Awkward?

Old? Very young?

Healthy? Unhealthy?

Sluggish? High energy? Low energy?

How does he or she sit, stand, or walk around normally?

When the character gets nervous, what does he or she do? What sort of little quirks? What sort of gestures with the hands? What facial expressions?

If the character had to run, how would it look? If the character had to dance? Fight? Get silly? Get frightened?

WHAT THE CHARACTER FEELS AND THINKS

The script will give you insight into the emotions and desires of the character, but plays are open to interpretation. You should discuss these aspects of the character:

What does he or she want?

What is he or she willing to do to get what is wanted?

What is the character afraid of?

What is he or she hiding?

What is the character's view of the world?

What are his or her responsibilities? Dreams? Hopes?

What emotions are most obvious in the character? Happiness? Sadness? Grief? Fear? Optimism? Depression? Anxiety?

What is motivating the character to do what he or she does? Money? Love? Power? Duty?

When you think about all this, the personality, physical appearance, and nature of the character will be clearer.

MEMORIZATION

The other major thing the actor must do to help the director and move the play rehearsals along is to memorize his or her lines in a timely fashion. This is easy for some and very hard for others. Somehow, though, it has to get done!

Here are some methods to share with your actors, and you may find others:

- DIVIDE AND REPEAT: Divide your play into sections, and memorize your part, along with your cues, one section at a time, and repeat, repeat, repeat! Add new sections to the ones you've already mastered.

- WRITE IT DOWN: Write out your lines in longhand, saying them as you write them down. The hand/eye/voice combination really helps to familiarize you with the ins and outs of each line.

- RECORD YOURSELF: Record your voice saying your lines. Have someone else (or you) say the cue lines as well. Listen over and over. (Don't use video; watching yourself doesn't help.)

- RUN LINES WITH A PARTNER: Have a friend, parent, sister, or brother run lines with you: they say the other lines, you say yours. Repeat, repeat, repeat. Aim to be "word perfect" and have your partner stop you if you miss things here and there.

Try all the methods. Regardless, repetition is the key. Eventually, the lines will sink in.

WRITING IT ALL DOWN

Either you or your stage manager must find a way to write down every move and cue in your show. How do you do this? Writing on each page of the script, you will take note of all the following:

1. Lighting cues

2. Sound cues

3. Movements of the actors

4. Movement of the scenery and the crew

I usually use a different color pen for each category of cues. There are only a few standard abbreviations:

ENT = entrance

EX = exit

X = cross

D = downstage

U = upstage

FF = full front

FB = full back

¼ R or L = quarter right, left

¾ R or L = three-quarter right left

PL/ PR = profile left, profile right

SL/SR = stage left, stage right

CC = center centerstage

CL/CR = center left, center right

Q1, Q2, Q3 = cue one, cue two, cue three, etc.

Find these and other words you will need and write them in the margins of your script on the lines in question. You might also use arrows, stick figures, circles, and so on.

Suggestions and Requests to Share with Your Cast

Tell your actors to carry a pencil (with an eraser) with them during rehearsal and to write down all their blocking notes. Encourage them to devise a shorthand that works for them, for example: "cross to the table at upstage left" would be "X to tbl UL" or "sit in downstage right chair facing full front" would be "sit DR, face FF." They may also want to use stick figures or arrows.

Tell them to write down suggestions concerning emotions or beats in the margins of their script and to name the beats. For example: "These lines are said mockingly." "These lines are said as I (the character) begin to fall apart." Suggest that they highlight their lines with a light-colored highlighter, and then write the blocking notes in a darker pencil in the margins.

STEP 5

PREPARING FOR A
PRODUCTION

*I do not stand in front of a cast and say "this is what the play
is all about." Because I really don't know. You find out when
you do it.*

JOANNE AKALAITIS, DIRECTOR

*If I am reading a play it affects me. I begin to visualize it as
I read it. It sparks many things—rhythms, tempos, images,
a sense of movement. They function together—all stemming
from the fact, the idea on the page.*

LLOYD RICHARDS, DIRECTOR

RIGHTS AND ROYALTIES

As you begin working on your show, the very first thing to find
out is whether you need to obtain permission to produce the
play and pay royalties. Your producer usually is in charge of this,
but it helps if you know the ropes—or you may be acting as your
own producer.

First, find the publishers of your play. The name will be
printed inside the script. If your play is in a book of several plays,
there should be information on the first page of the anthology.
The publisher or drama service needs to be contacted. They will
let you know whom to contact for permission. The licensing
house will need to know the size of your theater, the number of

performances you will be doing, and if you will be charging admission. Plays written in the United States before 1923 are in public domain, and royalties are not charged. However, if your play is translated from another language, the translator may need to provide permission. It is always important to check with the publisher first.

Not asking for permission can lead to serious legal consequences. Writers earn their living by writing, and royalties are the way they are honored and compensated for their work.

VENUE

Next, it is important to think about your performing space. You will need to get a concrete idea of the space and locale you will be using before you can continue planning. What sort of stage will you be using? How much backstage space is available? Are there dressing rooms? Storage space? Is there room to construct the set, or will that have to be done elsewhere? How large a space for the audience? How many seats? Is there a lobby? Will you want a lobby display for people to see as they enter?

THE PRODUCTION BOOK

I have, at the writing of this book, directed well over one hundred shows—full-lengths, one-acts, and musicals—and for each of them I had what I call a "production book." Keeping such a book helps me in several ways. It solidifies my ideas on how I will direct the show, and later, it acts as a record of what was created.

The production book goes with you to designers' meetings. It is the most vivid way of explaining your thoughts to those with whom you will be working. Often you can use pictures and non-theater-related ideas to express your interpretation of the play. Then the designers will get a sense of how you see the play, and they can take the suggestions back to their own drawing boards.

It will also have a copy of your budget to remind you of your spending limits.

The production book also goes to rehearsals. Eventually, you will have your blocking notes in the book, and you will make many changes as you go along. By the end of the rehearsal process, the book will tell the story of your work on the show.

Let's assume we will be putting together a production book for *The Rising of the Moon*. It will include:

- Table of contents

- Information on the author (bio, dates, and so on)

- Information on the publisher

- Royalty permission

- A complete copy of the script with room in the margins to write your blocking notes

- Your concept of the play

Concept means your vision of how the show looks and how it will come to life. At this point, you do not need to know *how* to get your ideas to materialize: You are using your imagination and sharing your ideas with your designers. What follows are various aspects of the production you need to consider.

- THE TIME PERIOD: Do you see it in the actual time in which it is set or in a different time? Do you see it in the country of origin? Do you imagine it set in another country at another time? Will it still honor the story and the author's intentions?

- THE STYLE: Is it realistic? Surrealistic? Imagine what the reality of the play is and the clearest way to represent it would be. Colors, photos, and reproductions of paintings will help your designers understand your vision of the play.

- THE GENRE: Do you see it as a drama? A comedy? A melodrama? Think about what the author is saying and make sure the genre is a true representation of that.

- IDEAS FOR THE LIGHTS: What illumination do you envision? Dark night? Where will the light come from? Streetlamps? Lighthouse? The moon? What kind of light? Rich? Ghostly? Blurry? Find more pictures that illustrate your idea of the light.

- IDEAS FOR THE SOUND: What sounds and sound effects do you hear? What music? Sounds of nature, water, birds, wind? Sounds of location, such as creaking boats?

- IDEAS FOR THE COLORS: Use paint swatches, squares of colored paper, bits of old magazines. Make a collage of what you imagine.

- IDEAS FOR THE COSTUMES. This is the provenance of your costume designer, of course, but you must be able to tell him or her what you see and what you imagine your actors will have to do physically in those costumes. Will they have to dance? Will they have to do fights, jumps, rolls? Since this is prior to your rehearsals, you can modify things later.

- PROPS LIST: List what you think is needed in the show. This will be a preliminary list since many more ideas will follow as you rehearse.

- PUBLICITY IDEAS: Feel free to include lots of photos that might symbolize your feelings. For example, if you see rich streetlamp light, a picture that you find in a magazine of a café at night or a reproduction of a painting by an artist like Van Gogh or Matisse could be used to suggest the colors or mood of the play. The play doesn't necessarily take place in a café at night: the images are just an example of the feeling you are going for.

- AUDITION IDEAS: Plans for tryouts, improvisations, or monologues that seem appropriate.

- CHARACTER THOUGHTS: Your first impressions of the characters in the play.

Remember: Symbols and imagery create the visuals of your concept. Fill your concept pages with as many examples as you can find. The play you are working on will evoke certain feelings in you, and without stepping on the toes of your designers, you will want to create some collages or collections of pictures that will express the feelings to them. The more ideas, the better. Even bits of music or poems or other such inspirations will help. It's important that you express how you see the play, because the designers cannot begin their work on the show until they know your concept.

Later, the production book will include:

- Prerehearsal blocking ideas that you want to try

- Official blocking notes (probably written in by your stage manager)

- Cast list and the role(s) each actor is playing

- Contact sheet with everyone's phone numbers (so you can find everyone at a moment's notice)

- Rehearsal schedule (including what work will be done on what night)

- Cues for lights and sound (a good way to notate this is underlining lights in one color and sound in another color)

- Final music choices, including music for preshow and intermission and bows

- Publicity information, including a list of newspapers, magazines, and radio stations

- Program notes: What you want to go into the program, including information on act one and act two, advertisers, bios of the cast and crew, pictures (maybe), special thanks to people or businesses who have contributed to the production or inspired you, and information on the play, the author, and other related materials. You might also want to inform the audience of the length of the intermission.

Finally, it will include:

- Copy of poster
- Copy of program
- Photos of the show

RESEARCH

Sometimes research is done by others to help you with your show. The dramaturg is one of those people. The dramaturg digs into all sorts of material on topics related to the play. In the case of *The Rising of the Moon*, he or she might do research on the political climate in Ireland in the late 1800s; the geography of west Ireland; Granuaile; the economy and customs of the times; the clothing, including the fabrics used; the agriculture; the police system and the court system (the assizes)—and more.

More often, you will do your own research. You may not want to look at all the past reviews or criticisms of the play. You may want to do a kind of abstract wandering through the play— just visualizing and using your imagination. But for concrete information, the library and the Internet are your two best sources. They can lead you to more specific areas of information when you need facts.

First, I try to find out everything about the writer. Who was she and what else did she write? What was her life all about and what was the main message she left to us in her work?

Then, I go to art books to research the look of the period. Who were the Irish painters at the time and what did their subjects look like? What style of painting was popular at that time?

I listen to the music of the period and the locale. I listen to dialect tapes of the region and try to scout out films set in the same area.

History books and books on politics, religion, and customs of the times are very important. How did people earn their livelihood? Were the police and local officials respected? What were the punishments for breaking the law? What sort of boats were at the dockside? What is the climate and what might the weather conditions have been at the time of this play? All sorts of related material can be found. There's a never-ending supply of peripheral material that can help you.

BUDGET

As with research, there may be others to set the budget for your production, usually the producer, but it is important for a director to know how to assemble, read, and comment on a budget and be knowledgeable about making changes and adaptations to keep things within its limits. Your sample budget would include the following items:

The Play

> Royalty (times number of performances)
>
> Scripts (one for each actor and for all the tech people; scripts will be either purchased, rented, or copied)

PAID PERSONNEL

> Director
>
> Assistant director
>
> Stage manager
>
> Assistant stage manager
>
> Set designer
>
> Costume designer
>
> Lighting designer
>
> Sound designer
>
> Scenic artist(s)

Properties manager

Props crew

Costume crew

Light-board operator

Soundboard operator

House manager

MATERIALS

Set construction materials

Set items (rented, built, or borrowed)

Costumes (rented, built, or borrowed)

Light instruments and gels

Electronics

Paint

Props, including food and perishable items

Music CDs

VENUE AND PUBLICITY

House rental per night (times number of nights)

Tickets

Programs (size of audience times number of shows)

Concession treats (cookies, drinks, and so on)

Posters and photos

HOSPITALITY

Party (after the opening night or after closing night?)

Gifts for the cast and crew

These elements can help clarify the many considerations that go into preparing for a production. Being organized is the key to keeping everything on track. If you, as a young director, have trouble with being organized, get help! Assistant directors, dramaturges, stage managers, and producers can help you wade through all the details, so be sure to include others in all the preparations, and don't hesitate to share the load.

STEP 6

AUDITIONS AND FIRST REHEARSALS

When you're directing, you can agonize but you can't indulge. Stuff has to happen.

TONY GOLDWYN, DIRECTOR

SCAN AND BREAKDOWN

One of the first ways to get inside the script and prepare for your auditions is to scan the script and break it down. No matter whether it is a one-act or a full-length play, sit down with the text and divide it. You can divide it several ways.

SCENES: You can divide a play by traditional scene breaks, as the author indicates. However, a great deal happens in one scene, so I don't think it's the best way. There's too much going on: mood changes, action, characters entering or leaving. Especially if this is a short play with only one act, your better choice is by French scenes or beats.

FRENCH SCENES: French scenes are sections of the act that are divided by the entrance or exit of a character. Every time a character enters or leaves a scene, that is the beginning of a new French scene. This term is inspired by the "well-made" plays of the French neoclassicists in the eighteenth century. Dividing a play this way creates variations in energies and tempos. Just as in real life, the energy changes when a new person enters a room. When a person leaves the room, the energy changes again, and the remaining people have a different dynamic. This is an exciting way to work scenes in rehearsals because you can concentrate on one small part at a time.

BEATS: Beats are sections of a play that signal an emotional change. Just as in daily life, feelings, situations, and reactions in a play change swiftly. A beat can be just a few lines or a few pages that you distinguish by a particular quality or emotion, which you name in the margins with simple phrases. You can label them by emotions: "These lines are expressing regret; these lines are expressing mounting terror," and so on. Or you can label them by ideas: "This section is like a peaceful lake; this section is like a wolf." Only you need understand what you actually mean by these words, and they will be very useful in rehearsals to get to the real heart of the material.

CHARACTER BREAKDOWN: Character breakdown is a way to track each character's appearances onstage in the play. Then you can get a clear idea of what limitations and challenges lie ahead concerning costume changes and exits and entrances as well as planning your rehearsals to use time to best advantage. For example:

Scene 1: Actors A, B, and C are onstage

Scene 2: A and B

Scene 3: B, C, and D

Scene 4: A, D, and E

Scene 5: D and E

When you do a breakdown for the whole show, you will be able to schedule rehearsals efficiently and not waste your cast's time. In early rehearsals, you may not want to go directly through the play from scene one right to the end; you may want to call the actors who are in selected scenes, out of order. Actor D and Actor E are not in the first three scenes, and you may not want to take up their evening if they will not be doing any work. Some directors do not wish to tie up actors' time in the early stages of the rehearsals. However, there are some directors who want to have the entire cast at every rehearsal so that they can understand every part of the process. How often you call your actors will be your decision.

AUDITIONS

Auditions are the true beginning of your hands-on work. Once you see whom you have to work with, once you cast your show, the play begins to breathe with life and energy.

You must first decide whether to conduct open or closed auditions. For either audition, have your audition forms available as your actors enter (see sample form on page 73).

You need a plan for evoking what you need from each actor. You know what your play requires, and you must try to bring that out in each auditioning actor.

Open Auditions

An open audition means that every one who is coming to tryouts will sit in the theater or auditorium together. Each actor has filled out an audition form and has a number. Actors may be called up to the stage one at a time, or a group may be called all together. Each actor does his or her monologue individually, and the rest of the auditionees watch quietly in the audience along with the director, the stage manager, and others who have been invited. When an actor has finished his monologue and the director no longer has any specific questions for him, he is free to leave or return to the audience to watch the rest of the process.

This style of auditioning has advantages and disadvantages. Many directors enjoy the community of theater workers present at an open audition. The production is "work," and all who become involved are "workers." Open auditions eliminate a star system: no one is featured above the others in the cast and the atmosphere is usually more relaxed and generous of spirit. The disadvantage is that the auditionees who go later in the day see

Sample Audition Form

Name _____   Audition # _____

Address _____

City _____   Zip _____

Home phone _____   Cell phone _____

Message _____

Height _____   Weight _____

Hair color _____   Age range _____

Are you willing to cut or color your hair? Yes __ No __

Part you are auditioning for: _____

Will you accept any part as cast? Yes __ No __

Are you interested in working backstage or house?
Yes __ No __

Previous acting experience (use back of form if necessary):

Dance training/experience:

Vocal training/experience:

Do you have times and days when you are not available
(use back of form if necessary)?

Do you have planned holidays or days when you will be
away during the rehearsals and performances (be specific)?

what is going on and have more of a chance to tailor their work to what they perceive as appropriate. Of course, they do not know what the director has in mind and may only think they have an inside track.

At an open audition, the stage manager or assistant director lets everyone know that they will be called later concerning callbacks. The time for callbacks is announced, and it is a good idea to inquire if there are any conflicts. If you are considering an actor and wish to call her back, inquiring as to availability lets you know immediately whether she can return. If she can't, you note that on the application and make your decision without further auditioning.

Closed Auditions

A closed audition is very different. Usually the auditioning actors wait in an adjacent room, and the stage manager calls them in to the audition room one at a time. Each actor is seen alone.

Many directors prefer this method. It allows the director to concentrate on one person at a time with no interruptions. It is a bit more intense and focused, and for the actor this type of audition may bring on a stronger attack of nerves. Some directors hope for this so they can see the way the auditionee works under pressure. Also, the way you work with one actor may not be the way you will work with another, so this allows you freedom without influencing the next person who is trying out.

In a closed audition, when the actor is finished, he leaves the theater and waits to hear if he is called back. If the director is sure of a particular actor, she may tell him right then that he will be called back. That saves a phone call, and you are sure the actor is free and available to return for the callback audition.

The Plan for Auditions

As you begin auditions, it's a good idea to have a plan for what you will do and what you are looking for. Let us return to the cast list for our play *The Rising of the Moon*.

Sergeant

Policeman X

Policeman B

The Ragged Man

You know you need four men. How do you envision them? (Maybe you have decided to use a woman in one of the parts. Will this work? What do you see as her character?)

Who is the eldest character? The youngest?

Who is the toughest?

Who is the most vulnerable or innocent?

Who has the most stage time?

What type of energy are you looking for in each character?

Do you want to use the Irish accent?

As you think about the play, make a list of the traits and characteristics in the script. I say in the script because I want you to stay open to the possibility of a range of physical characteristics that may stretch your conception of how the play will look. If you plan ahead of time that the Ragged Man has to be tall and thin, you may miss a short, stocky actor who has just the right inner traits and physical skills.

Be very alert as you watch the auditionees. Try various things with them to see if they take direction and can demonstrate a range of emotions and physical flexibility. Also, have some different strategies to try.

STRATEGY 1

If an actor has a monologue, after the first reading (hopefully not more than two minutes) have him try it differently. Change the circumstances or the emotions and see if he can handle the changes.

If you know you are looking for a an actor who can show inner strength for example, ask him to try to do his monologue with a situation that requires inner strength. Think of a situation and be specific: "You are grieving for a dead friend but have to go on with your duties with dignity and determination." Or, "You are a loyal and patriotic soldier who has just been told he is shipping overseas, and even though you are frightened, you must say good-bye to your family and go." Your actor will do his same monologue, but with the motivation of someone striving to maintain his strength.

If you are looking for an actor who can demonstrate anger, have him try the monologue with the motivation of a situation causing anger, for example: "Do your monologue again, please, as though you were ready to start a fight with a stranger who insulted you for no reason."

Whatever you are looking for in the character can be tried in the monologue.

STRATEGY 2

If an actor has come to the audition with a monologue that she forgets halfway through, do you give her another chance? That's up to you. Many director's will say, "Sure, start again." Others will say, "Thank you, but no."

My thought is that giving an actor a second chance is more productive. You might also say, "Hold your script but try to look up as much as you can and don't just read it."

STRATEGY 3

If an actor has no monologue, what do you do? Many times an inexperienced actor will come unprepared for the audition but wants to be considered. It is in your best interest to give that actor a chance, and I often bring some extra monologue material along (not the actual play but something similar) just in case. Then I ask the actor to take a few minutes to read the material while I look at another actor.

I also believe in improvisation. I might ask the auditionee to relate a dream he once had, or have him tell me a moment of his life that was very exciting or frightening or funny. Sometimes, just hearing someone speak and having him move around is all you need to decide if he is right for a callback.

How to Keep Control of the Audition

KEEP IT SHORT! No one should go on for more than two or three minutes, yet often an actor will have prepared a long piece that won't show you any more than you've seen in the first minute. Stop her! Say thank you and follow up with what you want to do next, such as trying it differently or letting her go.

SAY WHAT YOU NEED! If an actor is dancing all over the stage and you want to see him stand still, stop him and ask him to do just that. Or ask him to sit in a chair. Conversely, if he is very stiff, asking him to walk around or dance a bit is fine.

BE DECISIVE! If you ask an actor to walk around and she says, "I don't think the character would do that," what do you do? That has happened to me quite a few times. Once, I asked an actress to try her monologue with some laughter, as though she were very happy. She said, "My character would never laugh. She's angry in this monologue." Well, that tells me a lot. It tells me that the actress has one way of looking at a character. It tells me that she doesn't trust me to have her best interests at heart and that she is worried that she might look foolish. It tells me that she isn't willing to experiment with other possibilities for inter-pretation. Maybe she will change as we work together, but it tells me to be careful about choosing her for a role where I will have to spend a lot of energy convincing her to try new or different things.

BE KIND. It doesn't help to get impatient or become rude with auditionees. They are nervous and are preoccupied with trying to do a good job and get the part. You can be far more effective if you treat others as you wish to be treated. "Thank you," "please," and "you're welcome" go a long way.

CALLBACKS

Callbacks give you a chance to see the actors again. This time the field is narrowed, and if an actor is called back, he is being seriously considered for the play.

The actors you have called back should read from your script. You should prepare copies of key scenes and have enough to go around. You may also want to try some improvised work—have actors try scenes together such as an argument or a scene where they banter back and forth.

You want to see how they move, so add some physical work as well. Perhaps you can have them walk as they say lines. Perhaps they need to run or shadowbox or creep across the stage. You could ask them to dance or somersault or cartwheel. Have them do whatever movement will help you decide.

Sometimes, I line up all the actors whom I am considering for a particular part and just look at them, all in a row. Just looking at posture and energy tells me a lot. Once you have seen all you can see, thank your actors.

It is helpful to inform them when they can expect to hear from you. Give yourself plenty of time, but know they are waiting to hear. Usually, you will call the ones whom you have cast in the parts first so they can accept or decline the part. Should there be a problem, you might need to go to the next person on your list.

Do not inform the actors who did not get cast until you have gotten all the roles filled with absolute "yeses" from everyone. The reason for that is you might need to make changes if your first choices don't accept the roles.

REHEARSAL TIME LINE

Along with auditions, preparing your schedule is important at this time. You should be able to tell the callback auditionees when final rehearsals will occur, what the hours will be, and who needs to attend. Then, after you have cast your show you can refine the weekly rehearsals to incorporate various scheduling problems that the actors have indicated on their applications.

Sample Time Line

The following is a sample time line for a show. Let's say you have a six-week rehearsal schedule and three weeks of performances on Friday and Saturday evenings and Sunday matinees. This is a total of nine performances.

Since *The Rising of the Moon* is a one-act, there will be another play on the bill as well. Six weeks seems adequate, but this time line can be extended or shortened depending on your production.

FIRST WEEK (MEET TWO TIMES)

Monday 5–7 PM: read the play, full cast call

Tuesday 5–7 PM: read again, discuss, full cast call

SECOND WEEK (MEET THREE TIMES)

Monday 6–9 PM: character work, full cast call

Tuesday 6–8 PM: Basic blocking, Scenes 1 and 2

Thursday 6–8 PM: Basic blocking, rest of play

THIRD, FOURTH, FIFTH WEEKS (MEET THREE TIMES PER WEEK)

Various rehearsals: You select how many and which parts of the play include dance, combat, and vocal rehearsals as needed. Also schedule when the technical director starts to build the set and when the scene painters and props people have deadlines.

SIXTH WEEK (MEET FOUR TIMES)

Monday 6–8 PM: off book (all lines memorized completely)

Tuesday 6–8 PM: Scenes 1 and 2

Wednesday 6–8 PM: Rest of play

Thursday 5–7 PM: Run whole play; 7–8 PM costume parade

OPENING OR HELL WEEK (MEET SIX TIMES)

Sunday 2–5 PM: Cue-to-cue, no actors

Monday 6–10 PM: Cue-to-cue with actors, then technical run-through

Tuesday 6–10 PM: technical run-through, first dress rehearsal

Wednesday 6–10 PM: full dress run-through

Thursday 6–10 PM: final dress rehearsal

Friday: opening night

SECOND WEEK OF PERFORMANCES

Friday, Saturday 8 PM

Sunday 3 PM

THIRD WEEK OF PERFORMANCES

Friday, Saturday 8 PM

Sunday 3 PM: Actor call one hour earlier

Sunday 6 PM until finished: Strike the show

This is just one example. You can also get a blank calendar and fill in the appropriate squares, but in either case your best choice is to sit down with your technical director and your production team and map out all the weeks you have. Then count backward from strike, through opening night and final dress rehearsal, all the way back to your first rehearsal. That way you can logically plan out your time.

Once your cast has been assembled, you will fill in the times that certain actors have conflicts. That way there will be no surprises when an actor is missing from a specific rehearsal. Make sure you indicate what time actors should show up at the theater for rehearsals and performances. Most actors need at least one hour before the curtain goes up. They will need to do costume, makeup, and warm-ups, and also they will need to check their props to make sure everything is in order. The crew might need an hour and a half to check props, lights, sound levels, and sets and get everything ready for the actors and the audience.

FIRST REHEARSAL: WHAT DO I DO?

The day or evening of your first rehearsal is the most important of the entire process. It sets the mood and the tone for the whole rehearsal process and acts as an icebreaker among the cast, the crew, the director, and everyone working on the show.

Prepare

Plan what you want to accomplish and be aware of the time constraints. What is most important to achieve at this first rehearsal? It is very important to make a list of your objectives and then try to decide which are most important. The list and the approximate amount of time for each one may include (not in any particular order):

1. Introduce cast and crew (10 minutes).

2. Introduce yourself and talk a bit about your experience, if you have directed before. If this is your first play, be truthful and thank everyone for their support as you all begin to work together (10 minutes).

3. Discuss the play, its background, and why you selected it (10 minutes).

4. Discuss your vision of the production, the period of history, and the general look (10 minutes).

5. Have the set designer show the model for the set (10 minutes).

6. Hear the play read by the cast (30 minutes to 2 hours, depends on the play).

7. Plan the details of the rehearsal schedule (20 minutes).

8. Have actors measured for costumes (30 to 60 minutes).

9. Set up physical and vocal warm-ups for starting each rehearsal (15 minutes).

10. Do some improvisation or have some discussion around the themes and characters in the play (30 minutes).

Which of these seem the most valuable to start things off? Which won't work? All the topics on the list are necessary and certainly could be addressed in the first two or three rehearsals. The times are certainly flexible and are just suggestions. Divide the list up and use it for several early rehearsals.

My own particular favorite choices are the introductions (1 and 2) and the reading of the play (6) while I have everyone there. Not every rehearsal will have the entire cast present. But, the choice is yours and whatever you choose, do it with conviction and with respect for everyone. The way you address the group is very important.

Be Honest

Admit that you don't have all the answers yet. You may even be in a complete fog about the play. That's OK. But be decisive in how to begin and take pleasure in the whole process. This is your time to assume leadership and bring out the best in everyone involved.

Advice to the Cast and Crew

Ask that everyone please be on time to all rehearsals. On time means five minutes early. If an actor is literally "on time," he is probably late. Promptness is essential for successful rehearsals!

Bring a notebook to take notes. Ask that everyone be prepared and bring a pencil and a datebook to record rehearsal information. These things might sound too basic, but otherwise the first gathering of the whole group can get bogged down by small details.

Ask that everyone be really present. Leave other problems at the door and pick them up later after rehearsals.

And finally, trust the play. Remember that everyone is here to honor the play and be the bridge between the writer and the audience who are eagerly waiting to see your work.

STEP 7

Solving Specific Problems

The director must work to establish that a play well chosen and well presented is a peculiarly vivid art form which affects its beholders more strongly than reading. What is seen on the stage appears as visible evidence of some aspect of human life. The theatre, therefore, must speak accurately and truly. By reinforcing knowledge from other sources, competent theatre can help to create a thinking and sensitive community.

Marian Gallaway
The Director in the Theatre

All art is an intensification of life. Acting is not mimicry of life, nor delivering the lines of the dramatist. The art of the actor is to create out of himself the intensification of life which the dramatist has suggested in the power of the writing.

Kenneth Thorpe Rowe
A Theater in Your Head: Analyzing the Play and Visualizing Its Production

READINGS AND STAGED READINGS

You may be asked to direct or be in a reading of a play. What does that actually mean? There are two basic types of readings.

Readings

One is simply called that—a reading. By definition, that means a group of actors with scripts in hand reading the play either to a few interested people or to an audience. The actors sit on chairs and read their parts. They do not move around too much or use props, but they try to bring out the characters through their voices and the rhythms of the script.

Readings are useful for many reasons. They can be used as the first rehearsal of a production, to get the feeling for the characters and see if the casting has been appropriate. Sometimes after a first reading, the director may reassign parts to have a different actor play a different role than the one for which he or she was cast.

Readings can also be for the benefit of the playwright, so the writer can hear the script and get a sense of how it sounds off the page. Then the writer can make changes and rework certain parts.

Readings are also wonderful for radio theater. This is an art unto itself. As the director of a radio drama, you will cast actors with different voice tones and pitches so the listening audience can differentiate who is playing whom. You will also try to create different rhythms for different parts of the play to provide contrast and keep the listeners interested. You may also want to include a sound-effects person and music to liven up the drama. Often a narrator is included to read the stage directions and the action. The narrator's voice should be quite different from the other actors.

Readings are often entertaining to audiences just for themselves. People like to hear plays read. Often theater companies will have a whole series of readings over the course of a year, and these can be very popular. The readings can be the classics, works in translations, plays on a theme (such as war plays), plays by a particular author (such as the short plays of Edward Albee), or new plays by new authors.

Staged Readings

Staged readings are a little more complex, and you can make them a little or a lot more elaborate.

The major difference between a reading and a staged reading is that in the latter the actors are blocked to move around and approximate the action of the play. In some cases, the actors remain seated but get up on their lines, move a bit, then sit back down. In other situations, you might have them make entrances and exits or walk, sit, cross, or go up and down stairs as the script requires.

The actors might also wear appropriate costumes and use simple hand props that can be juggled with the script (teacup, fan, letter, gun, and so on). You might try for lighting effects and music as well. A narrator is still a good idea if you have elaborate stage directions.

This style is very entertaining to audiences, and there are many staged reading festivals for new playwrights as well as for classic plays that are brought back to life in this way.

One note: Be sure the scripts that your actors use are manageable, either bound or in a folder or loose-leaf book so the pages are easily turned and not flying all over the place!

READERS' THEATER

Readers' theater is an art form that takes a staged reading a bit further and is a legitimate and often elegant form of presenting plays with scripts in hand. It is sometimes known as chamber theater, story theater, or concert theater and is generally considered a way of staging plays in which the words are featured. Movement is minimal, and sometimes poetry and prose are used as well. Readers' theater can be an exciting way to bring all sorts of literature to an audience with just voices and gestures. As with readings, the audience's imagination is brought into the play creating the settings and the action. The audience and the reader together bring the script alive.

WORKING WITH PLAYWRIGHTS

If you are directing a play and have the luxury of having the playwright nearby, working together can be a helpful experience for everyone involved. The playwright might attend auditions to help with the casting of the roles. At the first rehearsals, the playwright might talk to the cast about the original ideas for the play, what motivations led to the writing and the deepest meanings of the script. An actor might ask about the character he is playing, and a lively discussion might follow about how that character can best be portrayed. After a performance, you might wish to invite the playwright and the cast onto the stage for a question-and-answer period with the audience.

I say *might* because this is a touchy area. I have worked with a lot of playwrights, and I know they have different ideas about how to be involved in productions. Before the twentieth century, many playwrights were actor-managers as well. They directed their own work, wrote for their own companies, and often acted in their own productions.

Now, it is different: directors usually make the ultimate artistic decisions on shows. A playwright often submits a script and then allows the director to take over completely. Sometimes a writer will want to have a great deal of input, just to make sure the director is on the right track. At other times, the writer wants to be surprised and lets the production team have complete freedom.

Then there is the other extreme. I once worked with a playwright who wanted to be at the audition, the callbacks, and every rehearsal, not only to watch and make suggestions but to videotape every move! Then I would get home, and there would be a long e-mail with notes. This was too much!

I think it is important that the director set guidelines about how much input is the best plan. When you and the playwright have agreed, everyone will have a good time. If there is no agreement, stress and strain will set in. Therefore:

- Have a plan of action about how you want to work on the script.

- Set guidelines and boundaries.

- Agree on how you will bring up suggestions for changes in the script.

- Invite your playwright to auditions and opening night.

- Include a short biography of the playwright in your program so that the audience knows the writer's credits just as they know about the actors and the production team.

ALTERNATIVE PLAYING SPACES

Theater can happen almost anywhere, and with careful adaptation and planning, you can achieve exciting performances in unlikely locations. You do not need a traditional theater space to do your play. The following are some alternative spaces that can be used.

- Church or synagogue

- Storefront

- Someone's home, front lawn, or backyard

- Outdoor areas, such as vacant lots, parks, bridges, parking structures, the beach

- Restaurants, kitchens (for kitchen plays!)

- Libraries and their lecture rooms

- Cafeterias at school

- Gyms

- Blocked-off side street

- Classrooms

There are many more I'm sure you can think of. I once had a directing student stage a one-act play in the local swimming pool. Another did a short play on a fire escape.

Once you've decided to do your play in some alternative space, there are some considerations.

- What does your script require? Will you need stairs? A flat area? A number of levels? Will it be indoors or outdoors? Can the script be made adaptable?

- What will you need to make it work? A hillside? A fountain? Will you need furniture to re-create a living room? A bedroom? A sofa? A table?

- How many people do you expect at each performance? How will you control the paying audience from the bystanders who show up?

- Will the audience be able to see and hear everything?

- Will there be places for the audience to sit down? To park their cars? Is there a restroom? Is the space wheelchair accessible?

- Can you depend on the weather? What preparations will you make in case it is raining or too cold or too hot?

- Do you have permission to use the chosen space? Have you found out what the rental fee will be?

- How will you set things up? Is there a backstage or costume-changing area? How will you stage entrances and exits? Are there electric outlets for lights and sound?

- If it is a public space, will you have inappropriate language that you may not want children to hear?

- If it is a public space, will you have stage weapons, like replica swords or guns? If so, and this is very important, you must notify the local police or authorities that you will be doing a play and you will have fake weapons. Otherwise, the police or sheriff's office may arrive and arrest your actors in the middle of a performance! (This happened to me and my actors once, and it was terrible!)

- Determine if there will be laws against charging admission. If you do a play in the park, is it subject to city entertainment laws? Entertainment taxes? What will be the noise levels?

- Are there obstacles in the playing area? You may need to adust your blocking to work around trees, pillars, altars, or doorways.

Alternative playing spaces can be very adventurous and provide the director, cast, and crew with some exciting challenges. Plan your performance as thoroughly as you would on a traditional stage and make your time line and preparations accordingly. The productions can be memorable, and audiences love the nontraditional approaches. Look around your town and think about the possibilities.

STEP 8

WORKING WITH PRODUCTION PEOPLE

Most sets give some indication of what sort of characters will inhabit the environment of the play. The designer normally uses set and decorative props as tools to achieve this effect. A living room decorated with inexpensive but reasonably tasteful furnishings suggests one type of occupant . . . the same room furnished with expensive but incredibly gaudy things indicates that a completely different sort of person lives in that room. If either were . . . littered with a month's worth of dirty dishes, clothes and other junk, it would seem likely that a completely different type of character was living there.

J. MICHAEL GILLETTE,
THEATRICAL DESIGN AND PRODUCTION

A successful play creates an imaginary world, a world molded out of the playwright's vision, a world into which the audience is drawn and through which it journeys. Production values—sets, lighting, costumes and sound—can heighten or undermine the audience's understanding and acceptance of that world.

LEE ALAN MORROW, *CREATING THEATRE*

WORKING WITH DESIGNERS, STAFF, AND CREW

Working with Designers

As the director, you must sit down with each of your designers to discuss his or her particular aspect of the show, and you have the responsibility to both talk and listen. You have your ideas on the play and you have your production book to share with them. But, you also want to listen to the ideas they put forth. This is creative teamwork and very vital to the health and artistic well-being of a production. Keep in mind that the director's main goal, at all times, is to interpret the writer's work and bring it to life in an honorable fashion. Designers are working artists, and they have wonderful plans and fantasies for the material you are discussing. It is your job to hold everything accountable to the main goal.

SET DESIGN

As you sit down with your set designer, there are certain things that you must make clear. Before he can begin to make your ground plan or model, you need to establish the following:

What do you see as the set?

How many scene changes are there?

How many different rooms or settings?

What do you want the audience to see?

What walls, doorways, or windows are needed?

Where do they need to be placed according to the playwright's demands?

What demands do you have for placement?

How high are the doorways?

What do you wish to hang on the walls?

What levels will be used? Stairs, platforms, risers, wagons?

Do you want an apron? Do you want to use the orchestra space?

Do you want to use just the stage, or do you want to incorporate the audience space in certain ways?

Where will the actors enter and exit?

What style of show is this? Realistic? Surrealistic? Expressionistic?

What does the style tell you about the look of the set? The colors? The materials to be used? (If you have a realistic wall, it will probably be made to look like brick or wood or wallpaper. If you have a surrealistic wall, it could be made to look like mirrors, clocks, puffy clouds, tomatoes, or just about anything.)

What budget are you working with, and can the show be kept within the budget constraints?

How long will it take to create this show, and are the deadlines reasonable?

Do you have a place to work and enough helpers to build the show?

Once you have expressed your ideas, allow your designer to draw, think, and dream about his own ideas based on what you have discussed.

You should request a ground plan and a sketch or a model within a reasonable amount of time.

LIGHTING DESIGN

Lights make your show. They can take the place of your set. They can create pools and spots and areas. They create mood and time of day and special effects. They can give you the illusion of time passing, dream states, fog, rain, forest glades, or the surface of Mars.

As you sit with your lighting designer, there will be some basic things you need to let her know so that she can get started. What are the requirements for each scene of the play? What time of day, what time of year, what weather? How much time passes in each scene? Does the sun set during a scene? Does a storm roll in? Does dawn come?

Discuss, also, the sources of light, the number of instruments the designer has to work with, and any special effects that will be necessary. Will there be "practicals" onstage? A practical is a lamp, or other small electrical device like a radio, that is turned on and off by the actors and not operated from the booth.

Discuss color. How will the colors chosen by the lighting designer mesh with the set and the costumes? Will you be using film or slides or digital effects? From where will they be projected? What sort of equipment and preparation will be required for this? When you begin discussing each scene, you may also want to talk about the degree of brightness, the saturation of colors (how pale or dark), and the use of shadows. Your designer may want to use gobos to create special effects. Gobos are metal slides cut into the shape of trees, jail bars, or any other design that can be projected on the flats or cyclorama to create scenery by means of light.

You may need other special effects or want some fun lighting. I've used flashlights, penlights, and Christmas lights in various shows for surprising effects. One show I did a while ago, *Failure to ZigZag*, a play about the sinking of the USS *Indianapolis*, has a scene that takes place in shark-infested waters of the Pacific Ocean after the ship has sunk. To achieve the underwater and in-the-water effects, the action was down in the orchestra pit and the lighting—blues, purples, greens, and turquoise—was focused into the pit. Just through the use of the lights, it seemed very realistic.

After you have spoken about the style, moods, and emotions of your show, let your designer go off and think about all this. She will have many ideas of her own, and you can begin to plan what will work at your next meeting.

SOUND DESIGN

There are three basic areas to concentrate on when discussing sound.

Music: There may be music indicated in the script, music for ambient sound (preshow and intermission), and any added music you might wish to include to set the mood or indicate a period of history.

Sound effects: Sound effects include noises such as car horns, crickets, dog barks, telephone rings, and cell-phone ring tones.

Special sounds: Special sound concerns include announcements, live microphones, and live music.

As you begin your discussion with your sound designer, be sure to include all information about the various sound requirements and the quality of each sound. What do you want your audience to hear? If a particular piece of music is indicated in a script, be sure you have permission to use that music. Otherwise, you may have to substitute something similar or omit the song altogether.

For preshow and intermission, it is advisable to select some sort of music that sets the mood that you want for the play. Discuss this with your designer.

For sound effects, make a complete list of what you think you will need. Of course, your designer will have many other ideas and suggestions. Once he hears your ideas, more will follow.

Do you want an announcement tape ("Welcome to our theater. Please turn off your cell phones")? Who will record this? Discuss this with the sound designer as well. If you are having live music or your actors need a microphone, discuss this.

Later, you will discuss duration (how long each sound effect or piece of music will run in the show), volume (how loud or soft it should be), and conclusion (whether it should end with a slow fade, a fast fade, or a chop). Also, plan for direction: where you want the sound to come from. If there is a radio playing onstage, do you want the sound coming just from the radio or do you want it to fill the whole theater?

Then the sound designer can plan a master tape or CD that will hold all the cues.

COSTUME DESIGN

There is a special connection between the director and the costume designer. The costume designer brings the characters, who are the heart and spirit of the play, alive and makes them believable. The director, in talking to the costume designer, sets out the basic interpretation of the play. Included in this discussion will be the time period in which the play will be set, the specific geographic location (topocosm), the classes of society that the characters represent, and the degree of realism that you are going for.

If your show is about a Ragged Man in nineteenth-century Ireland, he would have a certain look. Perhaps a tweed jacket and a cap. Most men in those days wore a collarless cotton shirt and a vest. The Ragged Man is not wealthy, so perhaps his clothes would have a worn-out look. The discussion then goes on to what the character has to do in the costume: dance? fight? fall?

If the show is modern, do you see the actors all dressed in formal wear such as gowns and tuxedos? Perhaps you see everyone in blue jeans and T-shirts. Modern shows can be harder to costume than period shows. Your costume designer will have to make sure things are accurate in all their details. For example, no one wore polyester clothing in the 1950s and everyone wore polyester in the 1970s. An audience will notice if the costumes are anachronistic or out of period.

Your job is to explain how you see the concept of the show and then let the costume designer go away to think, sketch, and imagine a set of looks for the show. She will want to know your color palette, including such basics as choices of loud splashy prints, solid colors, or muted natural tones. What statements are you making with the costumes? What do you want the audience to understand?

She will want to know whom you have cast in each role including height and weight of each actor, and then she will have to measure each actor, which includes head size for hats and shoe size. She will want a list of small hand props that may fall into the category of costumes, such as fans, jewelry, pocket watches, wristwatches, cigarette cases, parasols, purses, gloves, and the like.

Working with the Crew

How often have you sat through a play where the scene shifts were agonizingly long or really sloppy?

The director's relationship with the backstage crew can be the key to a smooth, well-run production. Assignments are usually filtered through the stage manager who has the direct line to the deck manager, running crew, dressers, and props people, but how you begin the tech rehearsals and how you communicate with everyone is vital.

What do you expect from the crew? How do you explain to them what you expect? Be clear and direct. Do you expect the scene shifts to be smoothly choreographed? If so, at least one added shift rehearsal will be needed, and the crew needs to plan for that well ahead of time.

Often on shows that require a well-coordinated team, I have asked my crew to do warm-ups either with the actors or in their small own circle. Warm-ups get them coordinated as a team and also help prevent injuries. The director's goal in staging the shifts is economy of motion. It should include:

- Working the crew as a team and having safety be the number one concern

- Efficient changing of scenery in as speedy a manner as possible

- Thinking that every activity is direct and smooth with as few exits and reentries as possible

The director must also communicate with the crew as to proper attire, including footwear. Traditionally, crew members wear black so they do not distract from the set, but sometimes they are dressed in the period of the play and are part of the cast in that way. Footwear should be soft-soled so that footsteps are not heard. Of course, the director and costumer may have different ideas.

PHOTO SHOOTS

Photography for a show is an important part of the preshow publicity in newspapers, posters, and advertising. During the run of the show, the lobby display might have photos of the actors for the audience to see. After the show, photos (or video, DVDs, etc.) are valuable both as résumé and portfolio information for the cast and crew and as an archive of the play for the director or the theater company to have in their libraries.

What has to happen at a photo shoot? Keep it simple. Know which parts of the play you want to photograph and select the actors who are in those parts. In your mind, decide which scenes are the most indicative of the play itself and come to the photographer with clear choices. Come prepared. Don't waste the photographer's time. Do not try to get the whole cast into a publicity shot unless it is a small cast. Have a large group photo later just for happy memories. Shoot in black and white, which is best for publicity. Tell the photographer in clear, direct terms what each shot represents and help the photographer get the correct expression and emotion needed. Work with the photographer on the digital imagery or the proof sheets and have him or her make suggestions on what looks best.

If there will be individual headshots of each actor, work with the photographer by introducing each actor. Inform your actors that they must be on time for the shoot, must listen to the photographer's requests, and must not come up with "better ideas" unless asked.

Have your actors bring the proper clothing and makeup to best represent the scenes being shot. Have them personify the characters as best they can and not waste anyone's time.

Encourage the photographer to say what he or she needs. It may be important for the actors being photographed to stay back or in another room while one particular picture is being set up. Ask your photographer for specifics, have him or her set up an action sequence or a pose that seems appropriate, but supply your own ideas.

Note that this is the photographer's territory, and he or she is in charge. The photographer may need extra time to set things correctly. Be patient.

PUBLICITY

Hopefully you will have lots of assistance for publicity for your show. But the director (sometimes together with the producer) is ultimately in charge of all publicity going out. You should ask to see the press releases and the photos, as well as proofreading the program before it is printed. Perhaps you will want to write the press release yourself. It should include:

- Who is producing the show (school, theater company, or individual)
- The name of the show
- The author
- The director
- The dates and times of the shows
- The location
- Ticket prices
- A brief paragraph saying what the play is about and if it is a comedy, drama, or musical
- Who it is appropriate for
- Some quotes praising the show from previous productions or reviews (if you have them)
- A publicity photo

Posters

The poster for your show should be approved by you and sent to the printer at least six weeks before a show so that it can be distributed in your area at least four weeks before opening night. Your poster should include:

- The name of the theater including the address and contact phone number
- The dates of the shows and the curtain times
- The place to get tickets, the prices of the tickets
- The name of the show
- The playwright
- The permission of the publishing company (by permission of _____)
- The director and any other staff members you wish to mention
- Some kind of graphic to catch the eye
- A line or two indicating if it's a comedy, drama, or musical
- The logo of any sponsors or grant organizations

Press Releases

The press release should be prepared at least four weeks before your show opens. Most local papers need a two-week lead on calendar information. Learn what the deadlines are for your target papers. Radio and TV community service announcements need at least three weeks, and large, city newspapers need four weeks.

A press release should include who, what, where, when, and why (see above) plus all the information that is on the poster (except the picture—you can include your poster with the press release if you wish). Be sure to underline the dates and times. Add a short synopsis of the play as well. Indicate if the show is for all ages, adult audiences, especially for children, and so on.

Photographs

Photographs should be taken at least six weeks before the show (with an approximation of the costumes since they will not be ready) so that they can be sent with your press release to the various newspapers in your area. If your press release has a photo attached, you stand a better chance of a featured spot in the newspaper.

Other Publicity Ideas

You may want to do some other things. These might include speaking to appropriate classes about the play, performing a bit of the play during an assembly or in the courtyard of the school or a public park, doing a radio or TV interview on a local station, or making billboards to put up in appropriate locations. Be creative and get the word out about the show.

PRODUCTION MEETINGS

Production meetings bring together the technical people of your show. It is a nice chance to sit down together to evaluate the progress of the production without the actors needing to be present.

The job of leading meetings may be either the director's or the production manager's, but the director should always decide who will be in charge and what topics need to be discussed.

Keep meetings businesslike and efficient and make sure everyone has time to speak. Decide how often you wish to have meetings and be consistent. Usually, during a rehearsal period for a play, production meetings are held weekly at a specific time when everyone can attend and when it does not interfere with rehearsals. Have an agenda of things that need discussion. Be positive and encouraging and think of problems as "creative challenges" and not stumbling blocks or brick walls. Make a list of things you wish to discuss. For example:

- Check-in from each designer on how things are progressing
- Budget
- Expenditures
- Schedules
- Materials
- Problems that have come up
- Plan for the week ahead

It is important to remember that successful production meetings make things go smoothly. They create a family feeling in which everyone is working together with goodwill and no major nightmares.

STEP 9

Your Role in the Actual Performance

Four weeks you rehearse and rehearse
Three weeks and it couldn't be worse
One week, will it ever be right?
Then out of the hat it's that first big night.
The overture is about to start
You cross your fingers and hold your heart
It's curtain time and away we go
Another op'nin . . . of another show!

COLE PORTER, SONGWRITER

HELL WEEK

This is the term usually given to the week before a show opens. I have also at times labeled it "hell fortnight" because that gives you two weeks to tear out your hair, cry, curse, and lose sleep. But, it is the most important time of your rehearsal process after your first rehearsal.

In the rehearsal time line, I mention that hell week will include rehearsals almost every night, and each night the show will improve as you achieve more and more of your goals. I want to elaborate a bit on what should occur during that last week or two before your play opens.

The Week Before Hell Week

The crew is learning the shifts. The actors are off book and know their lines. It will be helpful to have a prompter up until the last couple of days of this week. Set a firm deadline for no more prompter. After that, the assistant director might be the one to take notes on who has forgotten which line. She can sit with the script and circle things that the actors skipped over. After the last act, she can give notes to the cast on this aspect of the work, while the director gives acting notes.

Cue to Cue

This rehearsal is for the light-board operator, soundboard operator, and stage manager to coordinate all the cues. Usually the actors say the first few lines of a scene, then skip to the place in the scene where the next cue is about to come along. This is the best way to lock in the cues and make sure they are in the right place. In the case of sound, you will check for proper volume and proper duration as well. For lights, you will check that they are focused properly and have the right degree of illumination and the correct effects, such as shadows.

Technical Run-through

The shows starts. Try to keep going, but if there are mistakes in the tech, stop the show. This is not for the actors. They should be ready and able to assist the tech crew by being patient and being in the right place with the correct line. Usually the stage manager runs this rehearsal. The director takes notes and gives them after the last act.

Full Run-through and First Dress Rehearsal

Trying not to stop for tech, the actors now get a chance to work the show in costume. The designer and director take notes or stop the run-through only if necessary. After the last act, the director will give acting notes, and the designer will share her notes with the cast and listen to any problems the cast may have had with their costumes.

Full Dress Rehearsal/Final Dress Rehearsal

No stopping: Try not to stop for any reason. Many notes after the run-through.

During these final rehearsals, before opening night, it is helpful to give the cast and crew some final reminders.

REMIND THE CAST TO:

- Arrive at the theater in ample time to do everything they need to do without rushing.

- Check in with the stage manager.

- Check props and costumes.

- Listen to your requests for warm-ups.

- Take the time to get voice, body, and energy ready for the performance.

- Save small talk and being sociable with friends for after the show.

- Never eat or drink in costume! Bring a smock or robe. Try to limit drinks to water or tea.

- Think about someone to dedicate your work to and in the circle, even if you don't say it aloud, keep the thought as a calming influence.

- Read posted notes and try to incorporate them into that night's performance.

- Join the circle before the curtain goes up and be present as an ensemble member.

REMIND THE CREW TO:

- Arrive early enough to complete all precurtain tasks.

- Wear appropriate attire to the theater or have their blacks (or whatever they will be wearing) ready and waiting in a specific place backstage.

- Wear noiseless shoes (such as rubber soles).

- Check with the stage manager about other tasks that may need to be done that night.

- Do warm-up exercises: moving and lifting can hurt and can cause injuries.

- Attend the circle and be present with the actors.

OPENING NIGHT: WHAT CAN I DO NOW?

You have gotten through all the rehearsals, and it is now time for the audience to arrive and enjoy the show. From the director's vantage point, opening night is probably the toughest night of all. There are only a few more things that you can provide for the production, and after that you have to let go and let the cast and crew create their own magic.

That Afternoon

You can check the set: one last walk-through to determine that all is in place, including the set pieces, flats, set decorations, and props. You can hope that the paint is dry and check that the costumes are hung on their proper racks (although a good costume crew will have already done this). Has the stage floor been swept and mopped?

You can check with house management. Is the lobby of your theater space decorated properly to give the audience a feeling for the show as they enter? Does the lobby seem welcoming with information about the play and the actors. Is it clean? Are your programs ready?

The Evening Before the Show Begins: The Circle

Before the house opens, you will want to gather your cast and crew onstage in a circle. You might use this time for vocal and physical warm-ups and appoint someone from the cast to do this on future nights of the show when you might not be there or might not come backstage before the performance. We have already discussed warm-ups for rehearsals, but before performances, they should be kept very short, with exercises that do the job quickly and efficiently (unless dancing and/or singing is involved—dancers and singers need longer warm-ups).

This is also a good time for final well-wishings and "break-a-legs" to everyone. It is important that the director take the lead in this because the tone you set is the tone the cast will take backstage with them as they begin. If you are calm and confident in your manner and assume everyone is dedicated to excellence, that will leave a very strong, positive impression on a nervous group of actors.

I would include the crew in this circle as well. They are equally important to the play, for without them the flow, the changes, the technical movements would not occur. Having everyone warm up together keeps the ensemble in the same unified world, and the actors and crew will be able to sense each others' energies more effortlessly.

HONORING THE SPACE: Another reason for a preshow gathering is to honor the performance space, which will be the place where each one desires to do his or her best work. The theater space is often considered sacred—a place for highest achievements and noble efforts. Many times the director will say a brief thank you to the stage for being there so that the cast and crew can do their best.

HONORING THE WRITER: A dedication is often made to the playwright, without whom you would not have the wonderful words of the script to share with the audience The writer sat alone at a desk somewhere putting down these thoughts, and all too often we forget that in the hectic bustle of preparing a production.

HANDING THE SHOW OVER TO THE STAGE MANAGER: Opening night is the time for the director to officially give the show to the stage manager who is now in charge, for the director does not come to every performance (usually) and the stage manager does. The stage manager also knows every line, every cue, and every movement of the show and can give helpful notes or deal with emergencies. By acknowledging that formally, it is a way of telling the cast and crew that what the stage manager says, goes!

DEDICATIONS: Lastly, the company often may dedicate the show to family members who cannot attend or to people who may have inspired them to go onstage. The director may start this with a dedication, but usually others will join in. Not everybody does this sort of thing, but I always do. I feel it lifts the production up to its highest efforts and sets the mood for excellence. It also brings everyone into a serious and focused place. If I dedicate the show to my grandparents or to a favorite teacher who helped me along the way, I am setting myself a course that will be, hopefully, my best.

One more thing. Before the show, you might want to give your cast and crew gifts—usually flowers, a card, candy, cough drops (to soothe throats), bottled water, or some other small thank-you presents—which you can leave in the green room for all to see. Not every director does this, but I know it is appreciated when it is done. You don't have to go to a big expense. Even a hand-drawn thank-you card is fine.

LAST MINUTE NOTES: You will have given notes every night of rehearsal, and opening night is not the best time to make changes or suggestions that the cast cannot carry out without getting confused or even more nervous than they already are. Some directors, such as the famed German director Bertolt Brecht, are known to make changes even as the curtain is opening. But, as exciting as that may sound, I'm not sure that is your best plan. I often will watch the opening night show and still take notes, but post them in the dressing room the next evening in plenty of time for the actors to see them.

Now walk away! It is time for the play to begin. The best thing you can do now is take your seat in the theater and watch the show. Try to enjoy it, maybe take notes, maybe pray.

HOUSE MANAGEMENT

The director will, hopefully, not have to worry about taking care of front-of-house business. There should be other people to take reservations, sell tickets, usher, and see about refreshments during intermission.

If you are free of these obligations, you may choose to greet people as they come to the play, or you may just take a seat in the theater. You may also wish to hang out backstage until it is almost time for the curtain to go up so that you don't have to be a host or hostess. Whatever you decide is fine. There is no right or wrong here. You have done your best, and now you can hopefully relax.

If you have to do some of these front-of-house jobs, be friendly and professional and don't mix one role, as director of the show, with any other job. An usher ushers. She doesn't talk about the ins and outs of directing the play or all the crazy backstage goings-on.

You can also choose to have actors or crew members be ushers. The actors can be dressed in their costumes to set the mood for the play and greet the public, and this can be a lot of fun. As director, you will need to instruct your actors about how to behave. Do they greet the audience as themselves or as the characters they portray? This should be determined at rehearsal. If the actor is himself, he can chat with friends as they enter. If he is greeting the audience as his character, he must be professional and stay true to the nature of his role.

PRE- AND POSTSHOW PROTOCOL

The director and the stage manager set the protocol for both preshow and postshow. What follows are some suggested guidelines.

Preshow

- Actors arrive one, one and one-half, or more hours before curtain.

- Crew arrives two hours before a show (or what you decide).

- Actors and crew check in with the stage manager when arriving or initial the check-in board in the green room. (Do you have a board? If not, it is a wonderful way to make sure everyone has arrived. Make a list of everyone working on the show, with all the performance dates, then people initial the proper date when they arrive.)

- Costumes remain at the theater; actors arrive at the theater in street clothes.

- Actors must bring a smock or robe for makeup or for drinking or eating before the show.

- Once in makeup and costume, actors must not enter the audience area unless the director has planned it that way.

- Actors must keep backstage noise low so that the audience cannot hear them.

- There must be a clear boundary between actors' space and audience space. (Often well-wishers will want to come backstage before a show to give flowers or hugs. Do you want this?)

Postshow

- Actors, crew, and the director greet the public in the green room or lobby of the theater, not backstage. The director should establish whether the actors greet the audience in costume or not. It is preferable that the actors change clothes and make some attempt to remove their makeup before greeting the public.

- The director should inform the stage manager whether he or she will be coming to the following performances. The stage manager already has a contact list with telephone numbers in case the director is needed, but generally, he or she is then in charge of running the production,

QUESTION-AND-ANSWER SESSION

Does your show have a question-and-answer period after the performance? Usually the director or playwright (if present) will moderate this. Actors are often asked to return after their bows, sit on the set, and be present during this time. The director, or someone designated by the director, will set a time limit for the discussion, which hopefully will be helpful.

If there is going to be a question-and-answer session, the director might preplan a few questions to ask the audience. Sometimes audiences are shy to start things off, but once a few questions or comments are made, things get lively. The goal of a Q-and-A session is to get feedback that will be useful to the playwright or to have an energetic discussion about the meaning of the play and how it relates to the world around us.

STEP 10

CONTINUING YOUR TRAINING

"What is the way?" a monk asked his spiritual master.
"The way is your daily life," he replied.

ZEN APHORISM

Even a dog can be your master!

ALEJANDRO JODOROWSKY, FILM DIRECTOR

Anyone who wishes to can play in the theatre and learn to be-
come stageworthy. We learn through experience and experi-
encing and no one teaches us anything.

VIOLA SPOLIN, IMPROVISATION FOR THE THEATRE:
A HANDBOOK OF TEACHING AND DIRECTING TECHNIQUES

Assume that Ms. Spolin is wrong and right. She is wrong because there are many others who can lay the groundwork for
your education: writers who have published inspiring and com-
prehensive books on the subject of theater directing, teachers
who can set out scenes and plays to read and explore for your
continuing development. Other fine directors can lead you to
big discoveries just by watching their work—seeing their films
and stage productions or even reading their memoirs. And there
are many people who can inspire just by their words and deeds
even if we never meet them in person: personal role models and
heroes who give you the daring to go on. Parents, family mem-

bers and friends who have faith in us can provide strength and confidence to accomplish our goals.

But she is right, too. You have to be open to experience in order to experience. Life has to amaze you, all of it, especially the parts of life that raise questions—things you don't agree with, things that bore you or trouble you—so that you will look into them as well as into the things that you immediately enjoy. Your ability to experience life, to be aware and excited, is what will truly educate you. When you work in the arts, you make an agreement to be honest and to share your view of the world with others. And others are waiting to see what you see!

Audiences need you. We need your interpretation of life. Our world is changing so quickly that every artist's vision of life helps us to understand this world a little better. That is why we go to movies, museums, and plays. That is why we watch television, read books, look at photographs and paintings, and listen to music, all kinds of music—from the latest artists to the classics.

Your best training is to pay attention. You must get out there, fail, and try again; notice what works; deal with people; and experiment and reevaluate continuously. Compliments are great and we love them, but failure is a great teacher and not anything to be afraid of. The more you work, the better you will become. And, you must be your own teacher. Read everything you can. Find out what holds your attention. Really look at the world around you. How do you feel about art, music, movies, news, fashion, sports, science, politics—everything? It will all become a part of who you are; the richness and complexity and often the horrors and troubles of the world only add to the richness of your mind, spirit, and creativity.

15 PLAYS TO READ RIGHT AWAY

This is my short list of classic and modern plays that I believe are important to your understanding of good dramatic literature. Of course, it is very subjective, but I think you can't go wrong in having these as part of your library.

OEDIPUS REX by Sophocles (approx. 430 BC)

The finest example of Greek tragedy and considered the first murder mystery ever written, it is a perfect example of the writings of Aristotle's *Poetics* and provides a clear, highly concentrated example of dramatic structure and the unities of time, place, and action. It's also a great story.

THE BROTHERS MENAECHMUS by Plautus (approx. 200 BC)

The inspiration for Shakespeare's *Comedy of Errors* and many other plays about twins, mistaken identity, and comedy mishaps, this play is an important link between Roman theater with its social values, loose talk, and whacky coincidences and the brilliance of the later classical writings of the Elizabethan theater.

EVERYMAN by anonymous (1495 AD)

A brilliant morality play written, presumably, by a priest or nun during the fifteenth century, it is a tale of a man's last day on earth. Death has summoned him, and he has to prepare himself and look at who he is and what his life is about. The best example of an allegory told with vivid characters and powerful action.

HAMLET by William Shakespeare (1600 AD)

A huge canvas, several plotlines, shifts of time and place, wonderful, complex characters, and questions that are universal: loyalty, revenge, love, respect, honor, and self-doubt. The beauty of the poetry and the play-within-a-play make this a magnificent lesson in theatrical writing.

WOYZECK by Georg Buchner (1836, unfinished)

I consider this the first "modern" play. It is written in twenty-three scenes, which can be read and produced in any number of different sequences. The tale of a young soldier who is going mad, the scenes reflect the inner thoughts and his deteriorating mental abilities. The story is grim, but I recommend it for the brilliance of the writing style and the daring in which Buchner breaks all the rules. The playwright died of typhoid fever at the age of twenty-three and today is considered one of Europe's greatest writers.

THE WILD DUCK by Henrik Ibsen (1885)

Less well known than some of Ibsen's other plays, this is his masterpiece. It is a naturalistic play in which the secrets of the story are slowly revealed and the characters are asked to examine their values and ethics. The young girl, Hedvig, is the pivotal character, and Ibsen does not flinch from examining the hypocrisy and selfishness of the society in which she is being raised.

TRIFLES by Susan Glaspell (1916)

An early twentieth-century short play from a woman's perspective, it is set in the kitchen of an abandoned farmhouse. Wonderful characters, carefully detailed, and a fine use of subtext and psychological motivation. Subtle and dynamic writing with a rural American setting.

OUR TOWN by Thornton Wilder (1938)

One of America's most beautiful plays written in a seminarrative style, it attempts to celebrate the small, beautiful moments of our lives and tells its story through the memories of the deceased villagers of a New Hampshire town. No props, few set pieces, and pantomime to bring the action alive—spare and elegant.

DEATH OF A SALESMAN by Arthur Miller (1949)

America's greatest play. A man, his wife, his two sons, and a number of other business and family associates interact in a surrealistic drama that moves between the present and the past. Characters move through walls and through time; the play is actually the story of America, how it has changed and what values we hold as important. Heartbreaking and amazing with wonderful dialogue and memorable action.

RASHOMON by Fay and Michael Kanin (1950)

Based on the short stories of Akutagawa Ryunosuke, the play is a tale of a samurai, his new bride, and a bandit. It is a thrilling story of swashbuckling, jealousy, murder, and the truth. It is told three times, with a different perspective each time. What is the truth? Whom do we blame? Can we trust our own eyes? A play that can be done in many styles and with many variations.

WAITING FOR GODOT by Samuel Beckett (1953)

The most important play of the Absurdist movement. Set in nowhere and nothing happens. Brilliant characters and brilliant action. Can be a fine springboard for interpretation and discussion, especially about concept and worldview.

RAISIN IN THE SUN by Lorraine Hansberry (1959)

South side Chicago, 1950s, with racial unrest, housing discrimination and a society that is filled with intolerance. This is a beautifully written play with every character capable of respect and empathy. Written as a "well-made" play, you can trace the arc of the action and watch how the tensions build and eventually resolve. The play provides many viewpoints about its themes and ideas.

MASTER HAROLD AND THE BOYS by Athol Fugard (1982)

A beautiful play written by a South African playwright, it speaks of apartheid and the false boundaries between people that create class and race struggles. A timeless work with issues that are as fresh and important as when the play was first written.

MY VISITS WITH MGM (MY GRANDMOTHER MARTA) by Edit Villareal (1989)

A bilingual comedy-drama in short scenes chronicling the lives of three generations of women who have emigrated from Mexico and settled in the United States. Time past and time present and several stories of the family are all interwoven. The style is exciting and the characters memorable.

THE LARAMIE PROJECT by Moises Kaufman and the Tectonic Theater Project (2002)

Fascinating contemporary drama in documentary style about the 1998 murder of Matthew Shepard in Wyoming, a murder considered to be a homophobic hate crime. The story is harrowing and important, but I also put it on this short list because it is a wonderful example of a docudrama created from interviews and stories by the people originally involved. Eight actors play sixty roles, and the writing style is unique, having "moments" instead of scenes.

SUGGESTED READING

This section includes only a few of the many wonderful books on theater that are available to you. It's really another sort of list—that of materials on peripheral subjects that will add to your training in a more general way, related subjects that will help to broaden your education and ultimately help your theater work.

Acting

Brestoff, Richard. *The Great Acting Teachers and Their Methods.* Hanover: Smith and Kraus, Inc., 1995

Carnovsky, Morris. *The Actor's Eye.* New York: Performing Arts, 1984.

Chaikin, Joseph. *The Presence of the Actor.* New York: Atheneum, 1980.

Chekhov, Michael. *To the Actor.* New York: Harper & Row, 1953.

Hagen, Uta. *Respect for Acting.* New York: Macmillan, 1973.

Moore, Sonia. *The Stanislavski System.* New York: Penguin, 1960.

Silverberg, Larry. *The Sanford Meisner Approach: Workbook Volumes 1–4.* Hanover: Smith and Kraus, Inc., 2000.

Suzuki, Tadashi. *The Way of Acting.* New York: Theater Communications Group, 1986.

Art

Frazier, Nancy. *The Penguin Concise Dictionary of Art History*. New York: Penguin, 2000.

One Planet: See It for Yourself. Victoria, Australia, and Oakland, Calif.: Lonely Planet Publications, 2003.

Time-Life Books editors. *Seven Centuries of Art: Survey and Index*. New York: Time-Life Books, 1970.

The Art of Playwriting

Kennedy, Adrienne. *People Who Led to My Plays*. New York: Theatre Communications Group, 1987.

Pike, Frank, and Thomas G. Dunn. *The Playwright's Handbook*, New York: Plume/Penguin, 1985.

Spencer, Stuart. *The Playwright's Guidebook*. New York: Faber and Faber, 2002.

van Itallie, Jean-Claude. *The Playwright's Workbook*. New York: Applause, 1997.

Auditioning

Friedman, Ginger Howard. *Callback: How to Prepare for the Callback to Succeed in Getting the Part*. New York: Bantam Books, 1993.

Shurtleff, Michael. *Audition*. New York: Bantam Books, 1980.

Business and Basics

Hartnoll, Phyllis, ed. *The Oxford Companion to the Theatre*. London: Oxford University Press, 1957.

Stage Directors and Choreographers Foundation. *The Stage Directors Handbook: Opportunities for Directors and Choreographers*. New York: Theatre Communications Group, 1998.

Taylor, John Russell. *The Penguin Dictionary of the Theatre.* New York and London: Penguin, 1966.

Costume History

Batterby, Michael and Adrian. *Mirror, Mirror: A Social History of Fashion.* New York: Holt, Rinehart & Winston, 1977.

Cosgrave, Browyn. *The Complete History of Costume and Fashion: From Ancient Egypt to the Present Day.* New York: Checkmark Books, 2001.

Covey, Liz, and Rosemary Ingham. *The Costume Designer's Handbook: A Complete Guide for Amateur and Professional Costume Designers.* London: Heinemann Educational Books, 1992.

Davenport, Mila. *The Book of Costume.* New York: Crown Books, 1964.

Creativity

Barron, Frank et al. *Creators on Creating.* New York: Tarcher/Putnam, 1997.

Cameron, Julia. *The Artist's Way.* New York: Tarcher/Putnam 1992.

Herrigel, Eugen. *Zen in the Art of Archery.* New York: Vintage, 1999.

Morrow, Lee Alan, and Frank Pike. *Creating Theater.* New York: Random House, 1986.

Richards, M. C. *Centering.* Middletown, Conn.: Wesleyan University Press, 1962.

Dance, Movement, World Theater

Brandon, James R. *The Cambridge Guide to Asian Theatre.* Cambridge, UK, and New York: Cambridge University Press, 1993.

Horst, Louis. *Pre-Classic Dance Forms*. New York: Dance Horizons, 1937/1998.

Magriel, Raul. *Chronicles of the American Dance*. New York: Holt and Co., 1948.

Oxenhandler, Lynn. *Playing Period Plays*. Chicago: Coach House Press, 1959.

Scott, A. O. *The Kabuki Theater of Japan*. New York: Collier Books, 1966.

Zaporah, Ruth. *Action Theater*. Berkeley, Calif.: North Atlantic Books, 1995.

Design

Gillette, J. Michael. *Theatrical Design and Production*. Mountain View, Calif.: Mayfield, 1992.

Gloman, Chuck, and Rob Napoli. *Scenic Design and Lighting Techniques: A Basic Guide for Theater*. Boston: Focal Press, 2007.

Davis, Tony. *Stage Design*. Toronto: Theatrebooks, 2003.

Thornton, Peter. *Authentic Decor: The Domestic Interior 1620–1920*. London: Seven Dials Press, 2001.

Directing

Bartow, Arthur. *The Director's Voice: Twenty-one Interviews*. New York: Theatre Communications Group, 1988.

Bloom, Michael. *Thinking Like a Director*. New York: Faber and Faber, 2001.

Cole, Toby, and Helen Krich Chinoy. *Directors on Directing*. Indianapolis: Bobbs-Merrill, 1976.

Dean, Alexander, and Lawrence Carra. *Fundamental of Play Directing*. New York: Holt, Rinehart and Winston, 1980.

Koller, Anne Marie. *The Theater Duke: Georg II of Saxe-Meiningen and the German Stage*. Stanford, Calif.: Stanford University Press, 1984. ·

Film

Boggs, Joseph M., and Dennis W. Petrie. *The Art of Watching Films*. Boston: McGraw-Hill, 2004.

Dancyger, Ken. *The Director's Idea*. St. Louis, Mo.: Focal Press, 2006.

Proferes, Nicholas. *Film Director Fundamentals*. St. Louis, Mo.: Focal Press, 2007.

Improvisation

Hodgson, John, and Ernest Richards. *Improvisation*. New York: Grove, 1979.

Johnstone, Keith. *Impro*. New York: Routledge, 1992.

Spolin, Viola. *Improvisation for the Theatre*. Evanston, Ill.: Northwestern University Press, 1963.

Music

Copland, Aaron. *What to Listen for in Music*. New York: Signet/Penguin, 2002.

Readers' Theater

Coger, Leslie Irene, and Melvin R. White. *Readers Theatre Handbook: A Dramatic Approach to Literature*. Glenview, Ill.: Scott, Foresman and Co., 1973.

Stage Combat

Hobbs, William. *Stage Combat: "The Action to the Word."* New York: St. Martin's Press, 1980.

Hutton, Alfred. *Old Sword Play: Techniques of the Great Masters*. Mineola, N.Y.: Dover Publications, 2001.

Theater History and Literature

Alexander, Peter, ed. *The Complete Works of Shakespeare*. New York: Random House, 1951/1990.

Brockett, Oscar, and Franklin J. Hildy. *History of the Theater*. Boston: Allyn & Bacon, 2003.

Brook, Peter. *The Empty Space*. New York: Atheneum, 1982.

Cerf, Bennett, and Van Cartmell . *Fifteen Famous European Plays*. New York: Random House, 1943.

Clark, Barrett H., ed. *World Drama: An Anthology*. Vol. 1, *Orient, Medieval Europe, England, Greece, Rome, India*. Vol. 2, *Italy, Spain, France, Germany, Denmark, Russia, Norway*. Mineola, N.Y.: Dover Publications, 1960.

Cross, Wilbur, and Tucker Brooke, eds. *The Yale Shakespeare*. New York: Barnes & Noble, 1993.

Grotowski, Jerzy. *Towards a Poor Theater*. New York: Simon & Schuster, 1968.

Klaus, Carl et al. *Stages of Drama: Classical to Contemporary*. New York: St. Martin's Press, 1995.

Roberts, Vera Mowry. *The Nature of Theatre*. New York: Harper & Row, 1971.

APPENDIX

THE RISING OF THE MOON

Commentary on *The Rising of the Moon*

The Rising of the Moon was first produced at The Abbey Theatre, Dublin, Ireland, on March 9, 1907. The title is from an old ballad whose lyrics provided hope and faith to the Irish rebels of the eighteenth century.

> Death to every foe and traitor! Forward! Strike the marching tune.
> And hurrah, my boys, for freedom at the rising of the moon.

What follows are comments about the play.

"The Rising of The Moon," produced by the Abbey Theatre in 1907, is related to the struggle between the Irish Revolutionaries and the forces loyal to the British government, a conflict which literally set brother against brother for decades on end. It is interesting to note that Lady Gregory never explicitly states that the escapee is a revolutionary, yet the audience is almost immediately aware that the wanted man is not a criminal but a patriot.

RICHARD GOLDSTONE AND ABRAHAM LASS,
THE MENTOR BOOK OF SHORT PLAYS

. . . theatrically effective, The Rising of the Moon . . . is set on a darkened quayside and deals with the encounter of an Irish policeman and a fugitive political prisoner...

. . . The distinguishing characteristic of Lady Gregory's work is the distinctive folk dialect of Western Ireland in which she cast all of her plays. . . . That dialect influenced many later playwright . . .

JOHN GASSNER AND EDWARD QUINN,
THE READERS' ENCYCLOPEDIA OF WORLD DRAMA

. . . richness of idiom, the strong idiosyncrasy of character and sincere emotional power . . .

JOHN HAMPDEN, *24 ONE-ACT PLAYS*

A Short Biography of Lady Gregory

Lady Isabella Augusta Gregory (1852–1932) was an Irish playwright, a native of Galway, and a founding member of the Abbey Theatre in Dublin, along with the writers William Butler Yeats and John Millington Synge, who were her good friends. The Abbey Theatre directors were dedicated to adding dignity to Ireland and produced many plays in which the folk stories and myths of Ireland were brought to life.

A widow and a woman of privilege, she became very dedicated to the theater company and worked hard on all aspects of production, including writing plays and handling the business and management aspects, as well. In 1911 she led the company on a tour of the United States and was a strong and determined champion for Irish artists and writers using the rhythms and dialects of what is now known as Anglo-Irish.

The Rising of the Moon

BY LADY GREGORY

CHARACTERS *(In order of appearance)*
SERGEANT
POLICEMAN X
POLICEMAN B
A RAGGED MAN

Scene: Side of a quay in a seaport town. Some posts and chains. A large barrel. Enter three policemen. Moonlight. Sergeant, who is older than the others, crosses the stage to right and looks down steps. The others put down a pastepot and unroll a bundle of placards.

POLICEMAN B: I think this would be a good place to put up a notice. *(He points to barrel.)*

POLICEMAN X: Better ask him. *(Calls to Sergeant.)* Will this be a good place for a placard?

(No answer.)

POLICEMAN B: Will we put up a notice here on the barrel?

(No answer.)

SERGEANT: There's a flight of steps here that leads to the water. This is a place that should be minded well. If he got down here, his friends might have a boat to meet him; they might send it in here from outside.

POLICEMAN B: Would the barrel be a good place to put a notice up?

SERGEANT: It might; you can put it there.

(They paste the notice up.)

SERGEANT: *(Reading it.)* Dark hair — dark eyes, smooth face, height five feet five — there's not much to take hold of in that — It's a pity I had no chance of seeing him before he broke out of gaol. They say he's a wonder, that it's he makes all the plans for the whole organization. There isn't another man in Ireland who would have broken gaol the way he did. He must have some friends among the gaolers.

POLICEMAN B: A hundred pounds is little enough for the Government to offer for him. You may be sure any man in the force that takes him will get promotion.

SERGEANT: I'll mind this place myself. I wouldn't wonder at all if he came this way. He might come slipping along there *(Points to the side of quay.)*, and his friends might be waiting for him there *(Points down steps.)*, and once he got away it's little chance we'd have of finding him; it's maybe under a load of kelp he'd be in a fishing boat, and not one to help a married man that wants it to the reward.

POLICEMAN X: And if we get him itself, nothing but abuse on our heads from the people, and maybe from our own relations.

SERGEANT: Well, we have to do our duty in the force. Haven't we the whole country depending on us to keep law and order? It's those that are down would be up and those that are up would be down, if it wasn't for us. Well, hurry on, you have plenty of other places to placard yet, and come back here then to me. You can take the lantern. Don't be too long now. It's very lonesome here with nothing but the moon.

POLICEMAN B: It's a pity we can't stop with you. The Government should have brought more police into the town, with *him* in gaol, and at assize time too. Well, good luck to your watch. *(They go out.)*

SERGEANT: *(Walks up and down once or twice and looks at placard.)* A hundred pounds and promotion sure. There must be a great deal of spending in a hundred pounds. It's a pity some honest man not to be the better of that.

(A ragged man appears at left and tries to slip past. Sergeant suddenly turns.)

SERGEANT: Where are you going?

MAN: I'm a poor ballad-singer, your honor. I thought to sell some of these *(Holds out bundle of ballads.)* to the sailors. *(He goes on.)*

SERGEANT: Stop! Didn't I tell you to stop? You can't go on there.

MAN: Oh, very well. It's a hard thing to be poor. All the world's against the poor!

SERGEANT: Who are you?

MAN: You'd be as wise as myself if I told you, but I don't mind. I'm one Jimmy Walsh, a ballad-singer.

SERGEANT: Jimmy Walsh? I don't know that name.

MAN: Ah, sure, they know it well enough in Ennis. Were you ever in Ennis, Sergeant?

SERGEANT: What brought you here?

MAN: Sure, it's to the assizes I came, thinking I might make a few shillings here or there. It's in the one train with the judges I came.

SERGEANT: Well, if you came so far, you may as well go farther, for you'll walk out of this.

MAN: I will, I will; I'll just go on where I was going. *(Goes toward steps.)*

SERGEANT: Come back from those steps; no one has leave to pass down them tonight.

MAN: I'll just sit on the top of the steps till I see will some sailor buy a ballad off me that would give me my supper. They do be late going back to the ship. It's often I saw them in Cork carried down the quay in a hand-cart.

SERGEANT: Move on, I tell you. I won't have any one lingering about the quay tonight.

MAN: Well, I'll go. It's the poor have the hard life! Maybe yourself might like one, Sergeant. Here's a good sheet now. *(Turns one over.)* "Content and a pipe" — that's not much. "The Peeler and the Goat" — you wouldn't like that. "Johnny Hart" — that's a lovely song.

SERGEANT: Move on.

MAN: Ah, wait till you hear it.

(Sings.)

There was a rich farmer's daughter lived near the town of Ross;
She courted a Highland soldier, his name was Johnny Hart;
Says the mother to her daughter, "I'll go distracted mad
If you marry that Highland soldier dressed up in Highland plaid."

SERGEANT: Stop that noise.

(Man wraps up his ballads and shuffles toward the steps.)

SERGEANT: Where are you going?

MAN: Sure you told me to be going, and I am going.

SERGEANT: Don't be a fool. I didn't tell you to go that way; I told you to go back to the town.

MAN: Back to the town, is it?

SERGEANT: *(Taking him by the shoulder and shoving him before him.)* Here, I'll show you the way. Be off with you. What are you stopping for?

MAN: *(Who has been keeping his eye on the notice, points to it.)* I think I know what you're waiting for, Sergeant.

SERGEANT: What's that to you?

MAN: And I know well the man you're waiting for — I know him well — I'll be going. *(He shuffles on.)*

SERGEANT: You know him? Come back here. What sort is he?

MAN: Come back is it, Sergeant? Do you want to have me killed?

SERGEANT: Why do you say that?

MAN: Never mind. I'm going. I wouldn't be in your shoes if the reward was ten times as much. *(Goes on off stage to the left.)* Not if it was ten times as much.

SERGEANT: *(Rushing after him.)* Come back here, come back. *(Drags him back.)* What sort is he? Where did you see him?

MAN: I saw him in my own place, in the County Clare. I tell you you wouldn't like to be looking at him. You'd be afraid to be in the one place with him. There isn't a weapon he doesn't know the use of, and as to strength, his muscles are as hard as that board. *(Slaps barrel.)*

SERGEANT: Is he as bad as that?

MAN: He is then.

SERGEANT: Do you tell me so?

MAN: There was a poor man in our place, a sergeant from Bally-vaughan. — It was with a lump of stone he did it.

SERGEANT: I never heard of that.

MAN: And you wouldn't, Sergeant. It's not everything that happens gets into the papers. And there was a policeman in plain clothes, too . . . It is in Limerick he was . . . It was after the time of the attack on the police barrack of Kilmallock. . . . Moonlight . . . just like this . . . waterside . . . Nothing was known for certain.

SERGEANT: Do you say so? It's a terrible country to belong to.

MAN: That's so, indeed! You might be standing there, looking out that way, thinking you saw him coming up this side of the quay *(Points.)*, and he might be coming up this other side *(Points.)*, and he'd be on you before you knew where you were.

SERGEANT: It's a whole troop of police they ought to put here to stop a man like that.

MAN: But if you'd like me to stop with you, I could be looking down this side. I could be sitting up here on this barrel.

SERGEANT: And you know him well, too?

MAN: I'd know him a mile off, Sergeant.

SERGEANT: But you wouldn't want to share the reward?

MAN: Is it a poor man like me, that has to be going the roads and singing in fairs, to have the name on him that he took a reward? But you don't want me. I'll be safer in the town.

SERGEANT: Well, you can stop.

MAN: *(Getting up on barrel.)* All right, Sergeant. I wonder, now, you're not tired out, Sergeant, walking up and down the way you are.

SERGEANT: If I'm tired I'm used to it.

MAN: You might have hard work before you tonight yet. Take it easy while you can. There's plenty of room up here on the barrel, and you see farther when you're higher up.

SERGEANT: Maybe so. *(Gets up beside him on barrel, facing right. They sit back to back, looking different ways.)* You made me feel a bit queer with the way you talked.

MAN: Give me a match, Sergeant *(He gives it and Man lights pipe.)*; take a draw yourself? It'll quiet you. Wait now till I give you a light, but you needn't turn round. Don't take your eye off the quay for the life of you.

SERGEANT: Never fear, I won't. *(Lights pipe. They both smoke.)* Indeed it's a hard thing to be in the force, out at night and no thanks for it, for all the danger we're in. And it's little we get but abuse from the people, and no choice but to obey our orders, and never asked when a man is sent into danger, if you are a married man with a family.

MAN: *(Sings.)*

As through the hills I walked to view the hills and shamrock plain,
I stood awhile where nature smiles to view the rocks and streams,
On a matron fair I fixed my eyes beneath a fertile vale,
As she sang her song it was on the wrong of poor old Granuaile.

SERGEANT: Stop that; that's no song to be singing in these times.

MAN: Ah, Sergeant, I was only singing to keep my heart up. It sinks when I think of him. To think of us two sitting here, and he creeping up the quay, maybe, to get to us.

SERGEANT: Are you keeping a good lookout?

MAN: I am; and for no reward too. Amn't I the foolish man? But when I saw a man in trouble, I never could help trying to get him out of it. What's that? Did something hit me? *(Rubs his heart.)*

SERGEANT: *(Patting him on the shoulder.)* You will get your reward in heaven.

MAN: I know that, I know that, Sergeant, but life is precious.

SERGEANT: Well, you can sing if it gives you more courage.

MAN: *(Sings.)*

Her head was bare, her hands and feet with iron bands were bound,
Her pensive strain and plaintive wail mingles with the evening gale,
And the song she sang with mournful air, I am old Granuaile.
Her lips so sweet that monarchs kissed . . .

SERGEANT: That's not it . . . "Her gown she wore was stained with gore." . . . That's it — you missed that.

MAN: You're right, Sergeant, so it is; I missed it. *(Repeats line.)* But to think of a man like you knowing a song like that.

SERGEANT: There's many a thing a man might know and might not have any wish for.

MAN: Now, I daresay, Sergeant, in your youth, you used to be sitting up on a wall, the way you are sitting up on this barrel now, and the other lads beside you, and you singing "Granuaile"? . . .

SERGEANT: I did then.

MAN: And the "Shan Bhean Bhocht"? . . .

SERGEANT: I did then.

MAN: And the "Green on the Cape?"

SERGEANT: That was one of them.

MAN: And maybe the man you are watching for tonight used to be sitting on the wall, when he was young, and singing those same songs . . . It's a queer world.

SERGEANT: Whisht! . . . I think I see something coming . . . It's only a dog.

MAN: And isn't it a queer world? . . . Maybe it's one of the boys you used to be singing with that time you will be arresting today or tomorrow, and sending into the dock.

SERGEANT: That's true indeed.

MAN: And maybe one night, after you had been singing, if the other boys had told you some plan they had, some plan to free the country, you might have joined with them . . . and maybe it is you might be in trouble now.

SERGEANT: Well, who knows but I might? I had a great spirit in those days.

MAN: It's a queer world, Sergeant, and it's little any mother knows when she sees her child creeping on the floor what might happen to it before it has gone through its life, or who will be who in the end.

SERGEANT: That's a queer thought now, and a true thought. Wait now till I think it out. . . . If it wasn't for the sense I have, and for my wife and family, and for me joining the force the time I did, it might be myself now would be after breaking gaol and hiding in the dark, and it might be him that's hiding in the dark and that got out of gaol would be sitting up where I am on this barrel . . . And it might be myself would be creeping up trying to make my escape from himself, and it might be himself would be keeping the law, and myself would be breaking it, and myself would be trying maybe to put a bullet in his head, or to take up a lump of a stone the way you said he did . . . no, that myself did . . . Oh! *(Gasps. After a pause.)* What's that? *(Grasps Man's arms.)*

MAN: *(Jumps off barrel and listens, looking out over water.)* It's nothing, Sergeant.

SERGEANT: I thought it might be a boat. I had a notion there might be friends of his coming about the quays with a boat.

MAN: Sergeant, I am thinking it was with the people you were, and not with the law you were, when you were a young man.

SERGEANT: Well, if I was foolish then, that time's gone.

MAN: Maybe, Sergeant, it comes into your head sometimes, in spite of your belt and your tunic, that it might have been as well for you to have followed Granuaile.

SERGEANT: It's no business of yours what I think.

MAN: Maybe, Sergeant, you'll be on the side of the country yet.

SERGEANT: *(Gets off barrel.)* Don't talk to me like that. I have my duties and I know them. *(Looks round.)* That was a boat; I hear the oars. *(Goes to the steps and looks down.)*

MAN: *(Sings.)*

O, then, tell me, Shawn O'Farrell,
Where the gathering is to be.
In the old spot by the river
Right well known to you and me!

SERGEANT: Stop that! Stop that, I tell you!

MAN: *(Sings louder.)*

One word more, for signal token,
Whistle up the marching tune,
With your pike upon your shoulder,
At the Rising of the Moon.

SERGEANT: If you don't stop that, I'll arrest you.

(A whistle from below answers, repeating the air.)

SERGEANT: That's a signal. *(Stands between him and steps.)* You must not pass this way . . . Step farther back . . .Who are you? You are no ballad-singer.

MAN: You needn't ask who I am; that placard will tell you. *(Points to placard.)*

SERGEANT: You are the man I am looking for.

MAN: *(Takes off hat and wig, Sergeant seizes them.)* I am. There's a hundred pounds on my head. There is a friend of mine below in a boat. He knows a safe place to bring me to.

SERGEANT: *(Looking still at hat and wig.)* It's a pity! It's a pity. You deceived me. You deceived me well.

MAN: I am a friend of Granuaile. There is a hundred pounds on my head.

SERGEANT: It's a pity, it's a pity!

MAN: Will you let me pass, or must I make you let me?

SERGEANT: I am in the force. I will not let you pass.

MAN: I thought to do it with my tongue. *(Puts hand in breast.)* What is that?

(VOICE OF POLICEMAN X: *(Outside.)* Here, this is where we left him.)

MAN: It's my comrades coming.

MAN: You won't betray me . . . the friend of Granuaile. *(Slips behind barrel.)*

(VOICE OF POLICEMAN B: That was the last of the placards.)

POLICEMAN X: *(As they come in.)* If he makes his escape it won't be unknown he'll make it.

(Sergeant puts hat and wig behind his back.)

POLICEMAN B: Did any one come this way.

SERGEANT: *(After a pause.)* No one.

POLICEMAN B: No one at all?

SERGEANT: No one at all.

POLICEMAN B: We had no orders to go back to the station; we can stop along with you.

SERGEANT: I don't want you. There is nothing for you to do here.

POLICEMAN B: You bade us to come back here and keep watch with you.

SERGEANT: I'd sooner be alone. Would any man come this way and you making all that talk? It is better the place to be quiet.

POLICEMAN B: Well, we'll leave you the lantern anyhow. *(Hands it to him.)*

SERGEANT: I don't want it. Bring it with you.

POLICEMAN B: You might want it. There are clouds coming up and you have the darkness of the night before you yet. I'll leave it over here on the barrel. *(Goes to barrel.)*

SERGEANT: Bring it with you, I tell you. No more talk.

POLICEMAN B: Well, I thought it might be a comfort to you. I often think when I have it in my hand and can be flashing it about into every dark corner *(Doing so.)* that it's the same as being beside the fire at home, and the bits of bogwood blazing up now and again. *(Flashes it about, now on the barrel, now on Sergeant.)*

SERGEANT: *(Furious.)* Be off the two of you, yourselves and your lantern! *(They go out. Man comes from behind barrel. He and Sergeant stand looking at one another.)*

SERGEANT: What are you waiting for?

MAN: For my hat, of course, and my wig. You wouldn't wish me to get my death of cold?

(Sergeant gives them.)

MAN: *(Going toward steps.)* Well, good night, comrade, and thank you. You did me a good turn tonight, and I'm obliged to you. Maybe I'll be able to do as much for you when the small rise up and the big fall down . . . when we all change places at the Rising *(Waves his hand and disappears.)* of the Moon.

SERGEANT: *(Turning his back to audience and reading placard.)* A hundred pounds reward! A hundred pounds! *(Turns toward audience.)* I wonder, now, am I as great a fool as I think I am?

END OF PLAY

GLOSSARY

ABSURDISM: a style of playwriting that emerged after World War II and portrayed a world out of harmony with nature and devoid of purpose.

ACTION: what occurs in the play, the scene or part of the scene. Speaking, moving, or reacting are all part of action.

AD LIB: lines that the actor provides in a crowd scene or other unscripted parts of the play.

AGON: from the Greek, root of the word *agony*; the basic struggle that the characters go through in a play

ANACHRONISM: literally "out of time," indicating a word or phrase that may be too modern or a prop or set piece that is made from a material that had not been invented at the time of the play.

ANAGNORISIS: the moment of blinding clarity in a play where the main character has a life-changing awareness.

ANTAGONIST: central character in a play who is against the protagonist; a villain or a character who presents views and actions against the main character.

APRON: playing area onstage in front of the framed proscenium or curtain line.

ARC: the rise and fall of the action, energy, and conflicts in a play.

ARENA STAGING: nonproscenium stage; usually a full circle playing area with audience surrounding.

ATTITUDE: the way a character reacts to a situation in a scene.

BACKDROP: large area, usually of canvas, at the upstage portion of the stage where a scene is painted to indicate the location of the play.

BACKSTAGE: any area behind the playing space: dressing rooms, scene shop, storage, makeup, and so on.

BEAT: a feeling or objective in a part of a scene.

BLACKOUT: full dark onstage for one of several reasons, such as end of scene, end of act, or a moment dramatic suspense.

BLOCKING: the planned movements of the actors on the set in the play.

BREAKAWAY FURNITURE: designed to fall apart on cue during a fight.

BUSINESS: small movements and actions of characters in a play (such as sewing, cooking, reading the paper).

CATHARSIS: the cleansing feeling when the emotions of a drama bring about a clear conscience or a renewed spirit of serenity in both the characters and the audience.

CHEATING: turning out slightly from a profile position so the audience can see the actor's face more clearly.

CHEKHOV'S LAW: "If there is a gun onstage, it needs to be used before the play is over." In other words: if a prop is on the set, it should be integral to the play or eliminate it.

CHOREOGRAPHER: the person who stages the dances, fights, and other movement in the production.

CLAQUE: a friend or hired person in the audience who claps and cheers on cue to help energize the audience.

CLASSICISM: a style of theater in which order, balance, and respect for form predominate. Emotion is restrained and there is a strong moral vision presented in the work.

CLIMAX: the highest point of excitement, passion, or conflict in the play.

COMEDY: theater that evokes laughter and delight in the audience despite embarrassing or unusual situations; in spite of the trouble onstage, pain and terror are not present and the audience can relax and feel entertained without fear.

COMPLICATION: a situation of conflict in a play.

CONFLICT: a clash in the play; there are five basic kinds: person clashing with another person, person against society, person against nature, person against God or Fate, person against him- or herself.

CONTEMPORARY: of the time in which you are living and working.

COSTUME PARADE: first time the costumes are seen, usually under lights on the stage, so the director and designers can approve or make changes.

CUE: an indication that it is time for the other actor to speak or act—usually the last few words of the previous speech, a specific movement of another character, a series of musical notes, or a sound effect. A cue can also indicate a sound or lighting change.

DADA: a style of theater that mocked language and sanity. It employed nonsense words and wanted to show chaos and madness onstage. This early twentieth-century art movement preceded surrealism.

DENOUEMENT: the falling action toward the end of a play that provides the resolution and the ending.

DEUS EX MACHINA: Latin phrase literally meaning "God from the machine." The surprise entrance of another character who resolves everything at the end of the play.

DIALOGUE: spoken lines between characters in a play.

DOWNSTAGE: area toward the audience.

DRESS PARADE: same as costume parade.

DRESS REHEARSAL: an acting rehearsal with costumes.

DRESS THE SET: decorating a set for production.

DRESSER: someone who works backstage to help the actors with costumes and wigs.

DROP: a curtain or set piece suspended from the flies, which will descend during the play.

DRY TECH: a rehearsal without actors where the lights, sound, and set cues are set down on paper.

ENDOWMENT: the manner in which a prop is handled or treated in order to demonstrate a character's emotional state.

EXPOSITION: information slipped into the play about things that happened previously.

EXPRESSIONISM: a style of theater that shows the grotesqueries of life with serious but exaggerated characters and situations in order to demonstrate their inner life. There is a distortion of life usually shown through the eyes of the main character.

EXTRAS: actors who have nonspeaking, minor roles in a play

FARCE: comedy that is very exaggerated, with lots of physical action.

FLAT: a piece of scenery used to create a wall.

FLAT CHARACTER: an unreal or stereotyped character.

FLIES: an area over the stage in which set pieces, flats, or curtains can be hung.

FRENCH SCENE: a scene that begins when an actor enters or leaves, which creates a new dynamic in the play.

FOCUS: whatever holds your attention at the time.

FOURTH WALL: the imaginary wall where the audience is seated.

FREEZE: all action is stopped so that the audience can see the shapes of the actors in a particular situation.

GHOST LIGHT: light onstage for safety when all other lights are turned out for the night.

GOBOS: metallic slides used in lighting equipment to project trees, jail bars, venetian blinds, or other special effects two dimensionally onto a set.

GROUND PLAN: drawn by the set designer, a sketch or drawing showing the floor plan of the set, including the stairs, door-ways, walls, windows, chairs and tables, and so on.

HAMARTIA: the flaw in a character that brings about his down-fall, usually jealousy, pride, or other large emotions.

HOUSE LIGHTS: all the lights in the seating area of the theater (except the safety lights and exit lights).

HUBRIS: the sin of pride or arrogance in tragedies.

IMPLIED BUSINESS: specific action written into the script by the playwright (such as, "He picks up the telephone and makes a call").

IMPOSED BUSINESS: action invented by the director to enhance the scene of a play when none is provided by the playwright (such as having the actor sweep the floor or drink tea).

INGENUE: the innocent young-lady role in a play.

IMPROVISATION: nonscripted acting; spontaneous performance work.

JUSTIFY: to explain why you chose to do one thing over another. The way you feel inside justifies your outer action.

JUVENILE: the young-man role in a play.

KABUKI: Japanese popular theater using masks, music, and elaborate costumes and stories of samurai, the nobility, and commoners. A classical form popular for centuries with the theater-going public for the performances of the traditionally trained actors and the heroic tales they enact.

KILLING: getting rid of something on the set (like a table) or eliminating a light during a rehearsal to make things simpler and clearer.

KNAPP (or napp): the sound an actor makes either with his body or voice in a stage fight when striking a blow or receiving a punch or slap.

LAUGH HOLD: holding the next line until the audience has almost finished laughing at a funny line in a play so the dialogue can be heard and the audience has time to enjoy the humor.

LINEAR BLOCKING: to work on the show in order of the written scenes, from beginning directly to the end (nonlinear: to jump around, not in direct sequence).

MANNERS: the styles of behavior and speech in a particular period of history depicted in a play.

MELODRAMA: a play that blends comedy and serious drama and has clear definitions about good and bad characters.

MODERN: theater of the twentieth and twenty-first century usually incorporating ideas of science, technology, and psychology.

MONOLOGUE: speaking part for a solo actor to another actor, to the audience, or to someone unseen (such as God, the Fates, nature).

MOTIVATION: the reason why a character says or does something.

NARRATOR: one who tells the story to the audience; usually set apart from the other characters, but sometimes part of the story itself.

NATURALISM: a style of theater in which there is an effort to portray reality as close-up as possible, including the smells and sights of real life and discussion of all of life's natural functions, diseases, and intimate actions.

NOH: classical Japanese dance. Stylized dramas with music about "the floating world": stories about warriors, heroes, ghosts, and the spiritual world and staged with ritualized symbolism.

PALETTE: the range of colors to be used in a show for sets, costumes, lights.

PANTOMIME: dramatic or comedic action without words.

PASTORAL: a peaceful country setting in a play.

PLACES CALL: the signal from the stage manager that it is time for the actors to take there places for the opening of the show next act or a bell used by the house manager to signal the audience that the show is about to start.

PLOT: what happens in a play or novel or film; the story.

PLOTLINE: the story and its movement through the play; sometimes there are several plotlines in one play.

POINT OF ATTACK: the first hint of a problem in a plot; the first complication.

PRACTICALS: equipment onstage that works by being turned on by the actors, such as lamps, radios, or TVs.

PROTAGONIST: the central figure in a play, often the hero.

PULL: getting costumes, props, and set pieces from storage or neighboring theater companies.

REALISM: the style of theater that attempts to portray things and people as they appear to the impartial eye; a factual, truthful recording of details.

REPERTORY COMPANY: theater group that does several shows in rotation and often with the same actors in two or more plays.

REVERSAL: an upset or surprise in the play, a turn-around of events.

RISING ACTION: the build up of conflicts and situations in a play or film leading to a climax.

ROMANTICISM: a style of playwriting that puts emphasis on the noble heroic figure in a world of nature and mysticism. The world is seen as impermanent and essentially unknowable. Characters are on a search for freedom and kindred spirits and possess a passion for everything in life.

ROUNDED CHARACTERS: three-dimensional characters who have depth to their personalities.

RUN-THROUGH: a rehearsal in which you do not stop for changes or notes.

ROUGH BLOCKING: first rehearsals in which the director tries out the positioning of the actors. This is later subject to changes; a preliminary sketch, so to speak, of how the actors will move.

SAVE: a second actor jumping in and saying a line of dialogue to help the speaking actor who has forgotten a line.

SOLILOQUY: performed by a solo actor in which he or she is speaking to his or her inner self; different in this way from a monologue.

SIGHT LINES: the edges of visibility to fully see the action onstage; too far audience left or right may block visibility. Sight lines indicate where the action is still visible.

SIMULTANEOUS ACTION: two or more scenes going on at the same time.

SPECTACLE: the visuals in a stage set: costumes, lights, special effects,colors.

SPEED THROUGH: a rehearsal in which the actors say their lines very rapidly to test their memorization.

SPILL: light that hits an unintended part of the set and leaks along to another part of the stage.

SPINE: the main idea in a script; what the play is really about.

STAGE RIGHT: area onstage to the actor's right when facing the audience.

STAGE LEFT: area to the actor's left when facing the audience

STOCK CHARACTERS: standard, often clichéd characters who often appear in plays but have no unique features of their own, such as the butler, the nerd, the maid, the drunk.

STRIKE: after the final performance, tearing down the set, returning the props and costumes, and restoring the theater to its original condition.

THEME: a strong idea that appears as a main point of discussion in a script.

TOPOCOSM: the world of the play; the geographical location; the specific country, city, or town.

TURNING POINT: the place in the script where everything changes.

UNITIES: from Aristotle's *Poetics*—the unity of *time*, one day; the unity of *place*, one setting; the unity of *action*, one storyline, not several woven together.

UNIT SET: a set that can be used in many ways simply by rearranging a flat or changing the furniture.

UNIVERSALITY: that which appeals on a broad level to people of many lands and many cultures despite differences of language or customs. The grand themes of family, love, revenge, honesty, power, and such.

UPSTAGE: area farthest away from the audience.

VERISIMILITUDE (or verism): the factual representation of details as the artist perceives them to be the truth. May not be realistic. May be the reality of a dream or nightmare, but it is the truth as the artist or writer sees it.

WILLING SUSPENSION OF DISBELIEF: from Samuel Taylor Coleridge—what audiences or readers do when they experience a play or novel. They let go of the reality of where they are and enter into the world of the story.

WINGS: flats on stage right and stage left that hide the backstage areas from the audience and provide exits and entrances for the actors.

WORK LIGHTS: lights on the stage for general use.

ABOUT THE AUTHOR

W ILMA MARCUS CHANDLER is a theater arts teacher, director, actor, and choreographer. She was born in New York
and began her training at Bennington College in Vermont and
the University of Iowa, where she studied dance, theater, and literature. She went on to perform and teach dance and theater at
the University of Iowa, University of California, and Cabrillo
College in Santa Cruz, California, where she chaired the Theatre
Arts Department for many years. She has directed many plays
and play festivals and started improvisation groups, readers' theater festivals, and playwriting contests, as well as being co-chair
of the National Festival of Women's Theatre. She and her husband, John Chandler, live by the ocean in Santa Cruz. Her scene
study books and the ten-minute play anthology, *30 plays from
Eight Tens @ Eight*, have been published by Smith and Kraus.

Wilma Marcus Chandler's Directing Credits

FULL-LENGTH PLAYS

Agamemnon
*Angels in America, Part One:
  Millennium Approaches*
*Angels in America, Part Two:
  Perestroika*
The Art of Dining
Café Crown
Camouflage
The Chairs
The Crucible
Drinking in America
Everyman
Failure to ZigZag
Falling Back to Regroup

Frankenstein
A Friend in Need
God's Country
God's Favorite
It Had to Be You
Kind Lady
Laughter on the 23rd Floor
Laughing Wild
Little Murders
The Man in the Glass Booth
The Mousetrap
Museum
Playboy of the Western World
Poetry Reading

Rashomon
The Sea Horse
School for Scandal
Seven Keys to Baldpate
The Shadow Box
*Six Characters in Search of an
   Author*
This One Thing I Do
View from the Bridge
The Visit
*When Will I Dance?: The Life
   of Frida Kahlo*
Who Will Carry the Word?
Woyzeck

ONE-ACTS

The Hangman
The Heist
I Stand Here Ironing
The New Tenant
The Singing of the Stars

MUSICALS/OPERA/
CHOREOGRAPHY

Anything Goes
Apollo
Brigadoon
Cabaret
Carmen
A Dream Play
Grease
Indians

Kiss Me, Kate
L'Histoire du Soldat
Little Shop of Horrors
No, No Nanette
Octet for Winds and Dancers
Raga
West Side Story

STAGED READINGS

The Armchair Theatre Series
Con Game
The Dead Authors Readings
A Dull Pain Turned Sharp
Gifts and Curses
Louden-Nelson Reading
   Series
The Martin Luther King
   Project
The Video Haggadah
The Willing Suspension
   Series

FESTIVALS

The Dream Theatre Series
Eight Tens @ Eight Festivals
The My Kin Talk: Jewish
   Women's Theatre Events
The 12th Wave One-Act
   Festival
On Newest Ground One-Act
   Festival

Smith and Kraus Publishers, Inc.
Books on Directing and Producing

Anne Bogart—Viewpoints Ed. by Michael B. Dixon and Joel A. Smith paper isbn 1-880399-80-6 [978-1-880399-80-4] $14.95 / cloth isbn 1-880399-94-6 [978-1-880399-94-1] $35.00 pages: 208

Big Show, Tiny Budget by Sean Martin isbn 978-1-57525-569-9 $14.95 pages: 224

Can This Elephant Curtsey on Cue? Life Lessons Learned on a Film Set for Women in Business by Danielle Weinstock isbn 978-1-57525-568-2 $17.95 pages: 256

Dispatches from Armageddon: Making the Movie Megiddo by Michael York isbn 1-57525-311-9 [978-1-57525-311-4] $14.95 pages: 291

An Event in Space: The Rehearsal and Directing Techniques of Joanne Akalaitis by Deborah Saivetz isbn 1-57525-239-2 [978-1-57525-239-1] $16.95 pages: 232

In Other Words: Women Directors Speak by Helen Manfull isbn 1-57525-102-7 [978-1-57525-102-8] $19.95 pages: 185

Tips: Ideas for Directors by Jon Jory paper isbn 1-57525-241-4 [978-1-57525-241-4] $16.95 pages 263

The Path of the Director The First Ten Steps for Young Directors and Their Teachers by wilma marcus chandler isbn 978-1-57525-583-5 $16.95 pages: 224

Produce Your Play Without a Producer: A Survival Guide for Actors and Playwrights Who Need a Production by Mark Hillenbrand isbn 1-57525-255-4 [978-1-57525-255-1] $16.95 pages: 339

Provoking Theater: Kama Ginkas Directs by Kama Ginkas and John Freedman paper isbn 1-57525-332-1 [978-1-57525-332-9] $19.95 pages 340

For more information about upcoming Smith and Kraus books and special promotions, send us your e-mail address at info@smithandkraus.com with a subject line of MAILING LIST. Call to order (888) 282-2881 or visit us at SmithandKraus.com.